"It is encouraging to see my good fr [...]
Democrat, part company with Al Gore [...]
support the wealth-creating goals and a [...]
class. Wade has come out four-square for personal investment accounts
for Social Security reform. He is right. His party is wrong. And this book
is a good read."

—LAWRENCE KUDLOW, Chief Economist, CNBC.com

"Wade has tackled a complicated, controversial topic and cogently made a
case for a personal accounts-based public pension system. This is a timely,
well-researched book that deserves a close reading."

—TOM MARSICO, Chairman of Marsico Capital Management
and former manager of the Janus Twenty Fund

"I have seen firsthand in Chile, and in the ten countries that I have helped
to implement the Chilean model, what a system of Social Security choice
can do for a nation and its people. Such a system, if implemented in the
United States, would transfer power from the government to individuals,
enhance personal freedom, promote faster economic growth, and give even
the poorest worker the possibility of owning property in an individual retirement account. At the end of the day, it turns Marx upside down. Instead of
every worker a proletarian, it makes every worker also a capitalist."

—JOSE PIÑERA, architect of Chile's successful accounts-based pension
system and former Chilean Minister of Labor and Social Security

"Do you plan to grow old? Do you pay FICA taxes? If so, pay attention.
We're in for a national retirement meltdown unless Social Security is
fixed—and quickly. Wade Dokken's terrific and timely *New Century, New
Deal* tells us how to avoid an old age crisis and build retirement security
for all workers."

—RICHARD THAU, President of national Gen-X advocacy group, Third Millennium

"I am an adventurer. I love challenges. And I'm not someone who takes
no for an answer. That's why I loved Wade's book. Wade explains the
enormous challenge we face in saving Social Security. He offers a plan to
help all Americans create personal wealth. And he refuses to get side-
tracked by the naysayers in Washington. If you're ready for an adven-
ture—one that could create a mountain of cash for your retirement—
then this book is for you."

—STACY ALLISON, first American woman to reach the peak of Mt. Everest

NEW CENTURY, NEW DEAL

How to Turn Your Wages into Wealth
Through Social Security Choice

NEW CENTURY, NEW DEAL

How to Turn Your Wages into Wealth
Through Social Security Choice

A Wall Street CEO and Lifetime Democrat
Challenges the Washington Status Quo
On the Most Important Personal Finance
Issue of Our Time

BY WADE DOKKEN
President and CEO of American Skandia, Inc.

Since 1947
REGNERY
PUBLISHING, INC.
An Eagle Publishing Company • Washington, DC

Library of Congress Cataloging-in-Publication Data

Dokken, Wade.
    New century, new deal : how to turn your wages into wealth through social security choice / Wade Dokken.
        p. cm.
    ISBN 0-89526-211-8 (acid-free paper)
    1. Social security—United States—Finance. 2. Individual retirement accounts—United States. 3. Retirement income—United States—Planning. 4. Finance, Personal—United States. I. Title.

HD7125.D65 2000
332.024'01—dc21   00-062635

Published in the United States by
Regnery Publishing, Inc.
An Eagle Publishing Company
One Massachusetts Avenue, NW
Washington, DC 20001

Distributed to the trade by
National Book Network
4720-A Boston Way
Lanham, MD 20706

Printed on acid-free paper
Manufactured in the United States of America

BOOK DESIGN BY MARJA WALKER

10 9 8 7 6 5 4 3 2

Books are available in quantity for promotional or premium use. Write to Director of Special Sales, Regnery Publishing, Inc., One Massachusetts Avenue, NW, Washington, DC 20001, for information on discounts and terms or call (202) 216-0600.

For my wife, Susi Ann Dokken.

Your faith, your love, and your spirit are a balm to my soul.
You are my still waters and green pastures. May you for this life
and all that follows, be my companion.

For Andrew, Chad, and Blake.

The greatest wish of a father is for his son to be a greater man
than he. My heart is full and my life complete, for I know my
wish has been fulfilled three times over.

Table of Contents

WHY I WROTE THIS BOOK

SHORT OF WAR, NO ISSUE government can affect will touch the lives of the American people more than reforming Social Security. It is the single most important personal finance issue of our time, and the time for change has come.

Social Security turned sixty-five on August 14, 2000. It's time to hold a retirement party. It's time to strike a new deal for a new century. It's time to shift our focus from poverty prevention to wealth creation. It's time to turn every worker into an owner, a stakeholder in the greatest economic enterprise in the history of mankind.

As a lifelong Democrat, there's no question in my mind that tens of millions of American families have been well served by a system designed by one of our nation's greatest presidents, Franklin Delano Roosevelt. A man well acquainted with pain and suffering and hardship, Roosevelt vigorously fought to forge a New Deal with the American people and create a national safety net to protect workers, widows, orphans, and the disabled from a life of poverty and destitution during a tumultuous century of war, recession, and social upheaval. And that, as Martha Stewart would say, is a good thing.

But something happened along the way. Politicians started making promises they couldn't keep, spending money they didn't have, and raising taxes they didn't need. The government's bite started consuming 40 to 50 percent of a working family's paycheck. Consumer prices started skyrocketing on everything from housing to health care. Families started having trouble scraping together enough money each month to save and invest for their kids' education, much less for their own retirement. As a result, huge numbers of Americans became dependent on a government-run Social Security system to keep them out of poverty when they finally could make it to the finish line.

Now the jig is up. Nearly eighty million Baby Boomers are racing toward age sixty-five. And at age forty, I'm one of them. As a group—regardless of our political affiliation—we Boomers are beginning to sense that the light we see at the end of the tunnel isn't proof of the Promised Land but of an on-coming financial train wreck. We sense intuitively that structural design flaws mean the government-run Social Security system is in serious trouble, and we're beginning to conclude that we can't depend on the system to be there for us when we need it.

Guess what? We're right. Within a few short years—beginning around 2015, with a huge wave of Boomers retiring—Social Security will begin to shell out each year billions of dollars more in benefits than it takes in through taxes. Those deficits will mount rapidly into hundreds of billions of dollars each year—year after year—totaling upwards of $21 trillion in red ink by 2075. That's *trillion*—with a "t." The entire national debt right now is "only" about $6 trillion. So it's pretty bad.

The conventional Washington-knows-best options are grim. One option to cover the coming catastrophic costs of Social

Security, for example, would be to raise taxes dramatically. But that would slam the brakes on our economic growth, severely punish younger workers, destroy jobs and small businesses, threaten our global competitiveness, and very likely drive our country into a deep recession. Not good. Another option would be to cut Social Security benefits to the bone. But that would break a sacred social contract, rob people of the money they worked so hard to create over their lifetimes, and drive tens of millions of Americans into poverty. That is not acceptable.

The good news is that the financial world in which we live today is vastly different—and exponentially better—than the Depression-era environment of the 1930s in which our parents and grandparents grew up, the era when Social Security was created. Over the past seven decades, we've built a much stronger national financial foundation and developed savings and investment options to help ordinary people create extraordinary wealth. Products like Individual Retirement Accounts (IRAs), mutual funds, and 401(k) plans have stood the test of time. As the head of a $30 billion financial services company, developing and marketing such products has been my life's work. And I believe it's time to put similar financial products to work for all Americans, not just a select and privileged few. It's time to give *all* workers the freedom to direct a portion of their Social Security taxes into prudent, productive investments in the dynamic American economy through their own personal retirement accounts—new Social Security accounts very similar to private IRAs or 401(k) plans— so they can truly become stakeholders in the American experiment—now, in their peak earning years, before they retire, before it's too late. But persuading the politicians in Washington to embrace such commonsense change won't be easy.

There are heroes emerging in this debate on both sides of the aisle, leaders inside and outside of both major political parties who are rallying support for personal retirement accounts for all workers because they truly understand the benefits for working families. There are also demagogues on both sides of the aisle, leaders who bitterly oppose the creation of personal retirement accounts. Later in this book, I'll dish out praise, as well as name names and point fingers. Suffice it to say that the demagogues are on the wrong side of history. They are woefully out of touch with the dreams and aspirations of the American people. There is still time for them to come to their senses and do the right thing. But let them be warned. If they get in the way of the financial prosperity and retirement security of nearly eighty million Baby Boomers and their children—the forty-six million strong Generation X— they will be swept away by a tidal wave of voters who want a future of wealth, not welfare.

FDR himself, the father of Social Security, was a proud proponent of "bold, persistent experimentation." He saw Social Security as a beginning, not an end; a journey, not a destination. He publicly stated his desire to look for ways to improve and strengthen the program because his aim was to help people, not build bureaucracies. That's what this book is all about.

Nothing I call for in these pages violates the spirit of FDR's thoughtful, generous promises made so long ago. Indeed, what I call for will help us stay true to that spirit. It's time once again to become champions of "bold, persistent experimentation." It's time to put real *security* back into Social Security, and real security cannot be found by leaving working families dependent on a financial house built on shifting sand.

In the first part of this book, I describe the new economic and investment environment in which we live. I explain what I mean by "Social Security Choice" and why I believe personal retirement accounts will help working families create real wealth and financial independence—and find true retirement security in their golden years. I also lay out the essential elements of a well-constructed plan and answer questions people all over the country frequently ask me about this idea.

In the second part of the book, I appeal to the Democratic Party—my party, the party of my parents and grandparents—to wake up and smell the Starbucks. Times are changing and so must we. We must do more than simply repair an increasingly frayed social safety net. We must help build an escalator out of poverty, above and beyond the middle class even, and into the realm of unprecedented ownership and economic opportunity. We must shift our thinking from how to increase the minimum wage to how to help families maximize their wealth. And we must do so now, with a sense of urgency: Either the "party of the people" embraces Social Security Choice now, or it risks triggering a mass political exodus of tens of millions of working families, union members, single moms, African Americans, and Hispanics who want a new deal for a new century and won't—and shouldn't—take no for an answer.

Finally, I explain how workers all over the world are embracing a new investment-based approach to retirement security and how we can, too. And I will suggest it's time for you to make your voice heard in this vital national debate, a debate that promises to be one of the most important of our generation.

I believe that if we act now—with wisdom and resolve—there's no question that we can dramatically improve the lives of every American and can change history for the better. We can help workers making minimum wage retire as millionaires, or at the very least with hundreds of thousands of dollars more in their name than they'd ever hoped to have. But to do so, we must apply constant, consistent, maximum political pressure on the leaders of both political parties. We must make it clear what we want and why we want it. We must harass, harangue, and hound "the powers that be" into giving back to every American real control over his or her retirement savings. We must make absolutely sure that those in Washington with their big, fat, multimillion-dollar government pensions don't forget the working families who are paying far more than their fair share and feel like they're about to be left behind.

That said, I didn't write this book to run for office or become a politician. Government has its role in society. A good role. An important role. But let's be honest: Government doesn't create wealth; it consumes it. And that's not my mission in life. My mission is to help people create wealth. Not just people who have wealth today, but people who want to build wealth for tomorrow. I want to help people who have a little turn it into a lot. It's what I do, and it's what my company, American Skandia, does. And it's one of the biggest reasons why it infuriates me to see my own government treat working people's life savings with such callous disregard.

I wrote this book—in this way, at this time—to help win this essential, historic debate and make Social Security Choice and personal retirement accounts a reality for every man, woman, and child in America.

It's about turning wages into wealth.

It's about turning workers into owners.

It's about removing every obstacle that stands in the way of your success, happiness, prosperity, and security.

It's about making sure that every American—regardless of race, creed, color, sex, or political affiliation—has the opportunity to rise with the tide, not sink with the Titanic.

That's not asking too much, is it?

It's time for a new march to retirement security.

Chapter One

WHO WANTS TO RETIRE A MILLIONAIRE?

IT'S ALWAYS SO GLAMOROUS and exciting on TV. The flashy, futuristic set. The pulsating lights. The techno-pop soundtrack. The jam-packed studio audience—jazzed, trigger-happy, itching to go wild for a winner. The nervous, oh-so-normal-looking contestants—a mere three lifelines away from one million dollars. The enthusiastic host—always the optimist, rooting for the underdogs. And then, of course, the moment of truth: "Is that your final answer?"

Imported from England, *Who Wants to Be a Millionaire?* has become an overnight sensation in America, the most popular television show in U.S. history. Its host, Regis Philbin—for whom, you may recall, this is a second job—has become the Willy Wonka of wealth, the dream-maker of the digital age, a man *Forbes* magazine named one of the four most powerful celebrities in America.

What accounts for it all? It's not rocket science. We all want to see someone become a millionaire because we all want people to see *us* become millionaires. So we settle down with the kids and watch as people just like us drill for oil on national TV. We cheer them on, throwing popcorn in the air like confetti, rooting for them to become the next *People* magazine cover story. We play along with them, answering one question after another correctly and thinking, "That's it? That's all you have to do? Give me that phone. I'm calling that 800-number. I'm writing my ticket to the top!" These people are about to retire without a financial worry in the world. Surely we can, too!

Now, what's all this got to do with Social Security? Well, beyond all the *Millionaire* hoopla and hype, there's something very interesting going on. A new national ethos. A remarkable cultural phenomenon. Call it the Gospel According to Regis, though it goes much wider, deeper, and further than his show. It goes something like this: As we enter the twenty-first century, we're starting to suspect that it's easier than ever before to create wealth and financial security. Not *easy*, mind you, just *easier*. We suspect the rules are changing—for the better—allowing ordinary people to create extraordinary wealth. We're beginning to think that a safe, comfortable, dignified retirement—a blessing that may have eluded our parents and grandparents—may just be within our grasp, and none of us want to be left behind.

Guess what? It's not just a theory; it's a fact. In 1974 there were only 90,000 millionaires in the United States. By 1996 that number had grown to 3.5 million. By 1999 that number had grown to 5 million Americans with a net worth of $1 million or more. In fact, today, about 1 out of every 50 Americans is a millionaire, and rather than being concentrated in traditional wealth centers like New York, Boston, and Chicago, they live all over the country.

That's why books like *The Millionaire Next Door, The Millionaire Mind, 9 Steps to Financial Independence,* and *The Courage to be Rich* have raced to the top of the best-seller lists. It's not just books, of course. Walk into any grocery store and you'll see magazines with cover stories like "Score: Retire Early, Buy a Home, Pay for College, Preserve Wealth" and "10 Ways to Make Your First Million." Turn on TV these days and its seems you'll be just as likely to see an ad for an on-line stock trading company as one for a fast food company. Why? Because welfare is "out," and wealth is "in." Entrepreneurship is "in." Starting a small business is "in." Investing in the stock market is "in." Finding some way, somehow, to turn a little into a lot is definitely "in." And trusting Washington to give us a half-decent return on our Social Security taxes is increasingly "out."

It's not that we've all suddenly decided *en masse* that Gordon Gekko—the ruthless, money-hungry, pin-striped piranha in Oliver Stone's notorious film *Wall Street*—was right when he said, "Greed, for the lack of a better word, is good." It's not greed that's sweeping America (not all of America, anyway). No, what's really happening is that we're all coming to a new sense of realism about our financial futures—a rather commonsense conclusion, I might add—that our economy is in very good shape, our country is the world's only economic superpower, and our retirement is only a few short years away. So we'd all better make what we can, save what we can, and invest what we can, while we can, because otherwise we're all going to be in a heap of trouble. We're looking for new ways to create new wealth, new ways to build up a bigger nest egg for our "golden years," new ways to turn a little into a lot. And it's the right thing to do.

Indeed, this new sense of realism (particularly among those of us who are Baby Boomers)—that times are good, but time is short and retirement is approaching fast—is leading people to change their thinking fundamentally about wages, wealth, and what they expect from themselves and from government. It should come as no surprise, therefore, that in this new world of wealth creation the TV show *Millionaire* is so wildly successful. For we live in an age of explosive prosperity, a time unlike any other in human history. The question is: What do we do about it? Most of us aren't really pinning our hopes on landing a seat next to Regis. We're not delusional. But we are searching for ways to plug into the magic of the moment.

Which brings us, finally, to the intensifying debate over the future of Social Security. For the better part of a century, many of us saw Social Security as a reassuring safety net in an age of enormous insecurity, poverty, and war. But now we're entering a new century. A new century requires new thinking. We sense it's time for a new deal, a better deal. We certainly want a social safety net. No question about that. But many of us want more from our money than the government is providing. We expect more. And the Gospel According to Regis suggests that more is possible— much more.

My point: *It is now entirely possible for you to retire a millionaire— or, at the very least, with hundreds of thousands of dollars more than you would otherwise expect.*

You don't need to be a quiz show genius. You don't need to win a lottery jackpot. You don't need to get lucky in Las Vegas. All that would be nice, of course. But it's unnecessary. For if you were truly free to put a portion—not all, mind you, but just a significant portion—of your Social Security taxes to work for you and your family in the American financial markets, you likely wouldn't have to worry about your retirement. Nor would you have to worry about caring for your wife, husband, or children when you pass on from this life. You'd have what you need and then some. You'd also have the peace of mind of knowing your loved ones were cared for— well cared for—and that your lifetime of hard work really made a difference for their economic futures.

Now here's the rub: *The only thing that stands between you and a retirement nest egg of real wealth and financial security is politics-as-usual in Washington.*

Unfortunately, there are simply too many in our nation's capital with a vested interest in the status quo. They don't understand the magic of the moment; they don't get the promise of this prosperity. They will, therefore, bitterly contest the creation of personal retirement accounts. They will declare war on Social Security Choice. They will invoke the mantra that investing retirement money in a mutual fund or 401(k) is "risky business," or a "scheme," cooked up by a bunch of Wall Street sharks. Never mind that they believe in saving and investing for themselves, or that federal government employees have a wonderful retirement system where they can invest part of their income every month in stocks and bonds. To the demagogues, this isn't about fairness, after all. It's about politics! And as such, they will be moved to take action to defeat these ideas because so much of their own power and influence is at stake.

Make no mistake: The debate over the future of Social Security will be one of the most important—and contentious—we've had in our nation's history. It's going to involve everyone and their mother, literally. Because it's about the promises we've made to our parents and grandparents and how we're going to keep them. It's about the debt we've created and whether we're going to leave even more as a burden to our children. It's about the quality of life—and the quantity of wealth—we're going to have when we reach our "golden years."

Where do you stand?

Chapter Two

PETER LYNCH VERSUS UNCLE SAM

PETER LYNCH IS ONE OF the most famous and successful mutual fund managers in the world. You've probably seen him in those TV commercials with Lily Tomlin. He's "the Fidelity guy." *Forbes* magazine calls him one of the greatest minds in American business, and for good reason: Lynch ran Fidelity's Magellan Mutual Fund from 1977, when it was worth $20 million, until 1990, when it was worth $14 billion (now it's worth $100 billion). He retired at age forty-six, after helping the fund's value grow by 2,700 percent.

Lynch loves to point out how ordinary Americans have created extraordinary wealth over the years through mutual funds, Individual Retirement Accounts (IRAs), and 401(k) plans—not because they've become investment wizards themselves, but because they've wisely chosen to entrust their money to financial professionals who make it their business, day in and day out, to get the best return possible. Lynch should know. If you had invested $1,000 in the Fidelity Magellan Fund on May 31, 1977—the first day he began managing the fund—and never invested another penny in that fund, you would have had $28,000 on May 31, 1990, the day he left the Magellan Fund. Not bad, especially when you consider what a lousy return you're getting from Social Security.

Now, I'm not saying you're going to get twenty-seven times more money through Social Security Choice. What I am saying is that you're not being treated fairly by the current system. So, the real question is: Who would you rather have manage your retirement savings: Washington folks or professional money managers like Peter Lynch? If you'd like a significant rate of return on your money in order to build up a comfortable nest egg as safely and rapidly as you can—in other words, if you'd like to retire a millionaire—then the answer is obvious: Social Security Choice and professionally-managed personal retirement accounts.

How do I know? For nearly two decades—since I left the little ranching community of Towner, North Dakota, where I grew up—I've been in the financial services business helping working families save and invest for their retirement. Today, I have the incredible privilege of running one of the fastest growing financial services companies in the country, with more than $30 billion in client assets. Our customers include thousands of independent financial planners, accountants, and stockbrokers all across the United States. We provide them the tools they need to help their clients—including many middle-class individuals and working families in their late-thirties to late-fifties—create wealth, financial independence, and retirement security. Such tools range from mutual funds, variable annuities, and life insurance to investment-planning and tax-planning seminars to help people ask the right questions and find the right answers to meet the financial goals they have for whatever stage of life they're in. People trust us to help *them* make money. So it kills me to see what Social Security is doing with people's hard-earned tax dollars.

Where I come from, if something works, you stick with it. But if the status quo isn't delivering the goods, it's time to change course. At American Skandia, if we find a smart, new path that's good for our clients and their customers, we take it. We don't gamble. But we do take risks. Calculated risks. Prudent, well-thought-through risks. Ones that (hopefully) help people get a better return on the money they have entrusted to our firm. We give people a wide range of options. The more risks they take, the more money they can make. Depending on how much money they make, how much money they need, and how long they have before they retire, we assist them in developing a game plan that's right for them. But if there's one thing we flat–out reject in our world, it's a one-size-fits-all mentality. No two investors are alike, and it would be crazy to treat people as though they were.

One course correction we've pioneered, for example, was deciding that rather than manage people's money directly, we would manage the managers. Rather than create and control our own mutual funds in which we'd have a vested interest in recommending to clients (no matter how well or poorly those funds were performing), we'd instead act as unbiased talent scouts. We would help independent financial planners cut through the fog of choices to find the best-of-the-best mutual funds, which they could, in turn, recommend to their clients.

Every year, we screen the universe of 17,000 portfolio managers on a number of criteria, performance first and foremost. We then send our team out to the top asset management firms in the country to examine the best–of–the–best of these managers. We put them under the microscope. We give them the financial equivalent of a complete physical. We analyze. We scrutinize. We prioritize. We want to know these fund managers better than their doctors do. Do they make their customers real money year after year after year? Are they consistently getting better returns than their peers? What's their strategy? Are they consistent to their stated strategy? If they waver from a successful game plan—if they blink, if they divert, if they lose their focus and start to lose money—they're history. We want superstars. And that's what we've got—eighteen excellent mutual funds and variable annuity sub-accounts run by fifteen top-of-the-line money managers, with 725 years of combined investment experience, collectively managing over $1.5 trillion.

It makes sense, doesn't it? And it works. That's why our approach of managing the managers has been praised and imitated. That's why we win awards and industry recognition, and why Harvard Business School made us a case study. But far more importantly, that's why the financial advisors you turn to turn to us.

When you stop to think about it, the ability to create real wealth rather quickly in the stock markets—especially with the help of a professional financial advisor—is really quite astounding. Let's say you invest just $30 a week (an evening of pizza and Cokes for you and your kids or Chinese take-out for you and your spouse)—into a stock index mutual fund (one that will give you a similar annual return to Standard & Poor's index of the top five hundred stocks—the S&P 500). That's not really that much money—an annual investment of $1,560 a year. OK, so let's say you're forty and you start doing this each and every year until you retire at age sixty-five. Given that the S&P 500 Index has an historic return of 7.0 percent (since 1925), and factoring in the magic of compound interest over twenty-five years, you would have a nest egg of over a hundred grand ($105,575 to be exact) right when you need it most. Not bad, right? (And remember, you're probably paying a heck of a lot more than $30 a week into Social Security.)

Now, let's say you started investing small amounts of money like this when you were eighteen. Over the course of the forty-seven years of your working life, you would have built up a nest egg of more than half a million dollars ($549,541). Now that's *really* impressive—and infuriating—right? Just think what you could have done with an extra half million dollars if you'd only started investing thirty bucks a week from the time you were eighteen years old.

But see, this is the magic of the markets, the power of a personal investment portfolio—even a small one. There is no corresponding "magic of the Social Security Administration," and no amount of superficial tampering with the system will change that. Only Social Security Choice can change that.

At my company, we talk about the Rule of 72. It's a simple way of figuring out how long it will take to double your money in the market. It's a factor of the average annual rate of return you receive on your money, and how long you keep your money in the market. For example, if you invest $1,000 for ten years, you'll need an annual rate of return of 7.2 percent to turn that money into $2,000. Of course, if you only get a 2 percent annual rate of return, it will take you thirty-five years to double your money. Now consider this: The average annual rate of return in the U.S. stock market since 1925—even factoring the Crash of '29 and the Great Depression—is 7.0 percent. But Social Security's annual rate of return for most Americans is *less than 2 percent*. That's right—

| Rate | 100.0% | 41.4% | 26.0% | 18.9% | 14.9% | 12.3% | 10.4% | 9.1% | 8.0% | 7.2% | 6.5% |

1-800-SKANDIA   *www.americanskandia.com*

Ruler of 72

Read the number of years in which you expect your investment
to double. Check the corresponding rate you will need to earn.
For example, for your account value of $100,000 to double to
$200,000 in 10 years, you will need a return of 7.2%.

| Year 1 | 2 | 3 | 4 | 5 | 6 | 7 | 8 | 9 | 10 | 11 |

less than 2 percent. And that kind of horrendous return is one of the
main reasons it's time for a change.

After two decades in this business, I've found that the three keys
to successful retirement financial planning are:

- Getting started as soon—and as young—as possible.
- Getting good financial advice from a professional you trust—
  rather than going at it alone in a world of overwhelming
  choices and tremendous change.
- Getting the biggest possible return on your money—without
  taking unnecessary and unwise risks.

That seems simple enough, right? Common sense, right?
Absolutely. But you'd be amazed how many Americans don't follow such advice.

The fact is millions of Americans don't realize how *little* they
need to save and invest each month to build up a very sizable nest
egg by the time they retire. And what you don't know *can* hurt
you. It *is* hurting you. People think they need to be investing tens

of thousands of dollars into the markets to make real money. They don't have it, so they don't do anything. But thinking you need to have a lot to make a lot is pure myth. The truth is that you can turn a little into a lot if you get the biggest possible return on your money without being reckless and foolish. That's what saving and investing is all about. That's why it's so important to get good, sound, practical financial advice from someone who knows what he or she is talking about and can guide you through all the choices available to you.

That's why in the private sector—in sharp and vivid contrast to today's Social Security system—we've developed so many different kinds of investment options to help people maximize their money while minimizing their risks. No client has the same needs or desires. So the marketplace has developed different strokes for different folks. That's what my company has done. And that's why we're successful.

Am I a kind, gentle-hearted soul, eagerly helping the masses achieve their dreams of financial success and security? I'd like to think so. I'd like *you* to think so. But let's be honest. As Norm from *Cheers* used to say, "It's a dog-eat-dog world out there, and I'm wearing Milkbone underwear!" If I don't push myself and my team harder and harder to help our clients make real money—money they can see for themselves when we mail out their monthly statements—then my competition is going to chew me up and spit me out. They'll convince my clients that they have a better product, one that offers better returns at a better price with more free stuff thrown in for good measure. My clients will listen to them. They'll mull over the price of switching horses in mid-gallop. And they just might take the leap. And if they leap, I'm lost. The chances of my gaining back their trust is thin, at best. The next thing you know, sales are down, profits are drying up, share-holders are furious, the board is panicking, and I'm out of a job—sitting home, watching *Seinfeld* reruns, and identifying with that loveable loser George Costanza.

I don't run a government, and I don't run a monopoly. I can't force clients to stay with me. I can't force new clients to hire me. I can't tax people to get their money from them. I have to offer products and services that give people real value in the real world, or I'll get my real butt kicked. And I'll deserve it.

That's the power—and the justice and the beauty—of the marketplace. Help others win, and you win. Let others lose, and you lose. Nothing personal. That's just business. And that's the way it should be. The freedom for a client to walk away from me at any time—the freedom for a competitor to sneak up and offer my clients a better return on their money at any time of the day or night—has a wonderful way of concentrating your mind to do everything within your power and within the laws of the land to help your clients win.

Do investors understand that life has risks, that there are ups and downs in the stock markets? Of course. Do they understand their financial investments are not federally insured, not bank or credit union guaranteed, and may lose value? Of course they do. What they do not understand—and will not tolerate—is a financial advisor who is not fighting for their interests in the marketplace 24 hours a day, 7 days a week, 365 days a year. That is the unforgivable sin. And so it should be.

So here's my question: *Who the hell is running Social Security, and why haven't they been fired?*

It's not a rhetorical question. I'm serious. As I just mentioned, for millions of Americans, Social Security delivers an annual rate of return of less than 2 percent. Many get back far less than that. Some even receive a negative rate of return (that is, they will actually get back less in benefits than they put into the system in taxes)! Plus, there are huge risks associated with the future of the Social Security system because the government has made promises it can't possibly keep over the long haul. I'll get into the details of these two points—the pitiful rate of return and tremendous risks of the current system—in a later chapter.

Listen, if Social Security were a stock, you'd have sold it a long time ago. In many cases, you could do better putting your money in a simple passbook savings account than giving it to the government. In some cases, you could bury your money in your backyard or hide it under your mattress and do better than Social Security. In fact, if you dared come to me with a retirement portfolio made up of 100 percent Social Security, Inc., stock, trying to convince me that you'd made a good investment for the long haul, you'd find me jumping up and down on the top of my desk, screaming at you: "Sell! Sell! Sell!" So why exactly do we settle for financial incompetence at the epicenter of Social Security, our most important social safety net?

It's not Bill Gates and Michael Jordan and Oprah Winfrey and Steven Spielberg whose prospects for creating real wealth are being squandered by the dismal returns Social Security offers, or whose financial security is being put in serious jeopardy by the coming financial collapse of the entire Social Security system. The apples of Robin Leach's eye—the people who are profiled on *Lifestyles of the Rich and Famous*—are doing just fine, thank you. If and when they start to receive a monthly Social Security check, it will represent a mere rounding error in their checkbooks. So let them not be our concern.

Social Security taxes don't punish the rich. The risk that Social Security benefits might not be that secure doesn't keep the rich awake at night. The people who will take it on the chin for such lousy financial management are the tens of millions of hard-working, middle-class and poor Americans who depend—some of them solely—upon Social Security to deliver for them when they retire. It's their future that's at risk. It's *your* future that's at risk. So let's focus exclusively on how we can get you—and millions like you—a far better return on your money.

Seventy-six percent of American workers pay more in Social Security taxes than in income taxes. As a result, they are essentially depending on the government to give them a half-decent return on the money they've been pouring into the system all through their working lives. They deserve a decent, comfortable retirement. But we're all beginning to realize that it's not going to happen so easily. We're all coming to the painful conclusion that our government is poised to renege on promises it made, promises many Americans have depended upon, promises one wonders if they ever intended to keep—and there's something very unfair about that.

Forget Watergate. Forget Monica. If Washington doesn't move quickly and decisively to reform and save Social Security in a way that will truly keep the promises that have been made, it will be engaging in the biggest betrayal and scandal of all. I know from personal experience that there's a better way. There is a way to help workers get a better return on their money, to turn a little into a lot: by giving people the freedom to use personal retirement accounts. Washington may not yet get it, but some of us do. We're tired of all the political excuses. It's time to lead, follow, or get out of the way.

Chapter Three

THE POWER OF PERSONAL RETIREMENT ACCOUNTS

"WE SHALL MAKE THE MOST order-ly progress if we look upon Social Security as a development toward a goal rather than a finished product," wrote President Franklin Delano Roosevelt, in a letter to Congress on January 16, 1939, recommending "certain improvements in the law."

When Roosevelt signed Social Security into law on August 14, 1935, he wanted it to be a New Deal, not the Last Deal.

"We shall make the most lasting progress if we recognize that Social Security can furnish only a base upon which each one of our citizens may build his individual security through his own individual efforts," President Roosevelt continued. Indeed, he noted that "we would be derelict in our responsibility if we did not take advantage of the experience we have accumulated to strengthen and extend its provisions."

Progress and constant improvement was a consistent theme of the father of Social Security. On August 11, 1939, for example, FDR signed amendments to Social Security and observed that "we must expect a great program of social legislation, such as is represented in the Social Security Act, to be improved and strengthened in the light of additional experience and understanding." In fact, he urged an "active study" of possible future improvements.

It is in this spirit of "active study" and a quest for progress that I'm writing this book. The power of personal retirement accounts is that they represent a dramatic improvement in FDR's legacy and true financial security for all workers, based upon the "additional experience and understanding" we've gained as a nation over the past seven decades of saving, investing, and economic growth and development. Properly structured personal retirement accounts retain the basic contract of social insurance and build in a critical new factor—a way for ordinary people to create extraordinary wealth. Thus, they are fully consistent with FDR's goal of pursuing "bold, persistent experimentation" in the arena of public policy, while constantly reminding working families that careful, considered change is good, and "the only thing we have to fear is fear itself."

A personal retirement account in the context of a Social Security Choice system is similar to a private sector 401(k) plan or an IRA. It allows workers to have a portion—not all, just a portion—of their Social Security taxes deposited into accounts they own. Workers then can choose from among many professional, qualified, and licensed private sector financial services companies to help them manage their accounts and invest their money in the real, vibrant, thriving American economy. This can be done through a range of safe, conservative investment products such as stock index funds, mutual funds, corporate and U.S. Treasury bonds, and bank certificates of deposit. By taking such an approach, workers could then receive an annual return on their money of 6 to 10 percent or more, rather than relying entirely on the troubled Washington-run system to keep its promises over the long haul.

Any reform plan should be built on three simple yet fundamental principles.

The first should be **FULL PROTECTION FOR SENIORS.** We absolutely must completely and entirely protect today's Social Security system for seniors already participating in it and for people who will be retiring soon and have been counting on it. In other words, in no way can we pull the rug out from under people who have made their life's plans based on the current system, flawed though it may be. We can't raise their taxes. We can't cut their benefits, even by raising the retirement age and thus forcing seniors to work longer and harder than they had planned. The bottom line is that we must not do anything to shake the confidence of those who've worked hard and played by the rules. We are certainly wealthy enough as a country to keep our promises, and that's what we must do.

The second fundamental principle should be **FREEDOM OF CHOICE FOR ALL WORKERS.** This is what Social Security Choice is all about—the freedom to choose. Again, we must fully protect current and imminent seniors, but we must never force Baby Boomers or Gen-Xers into one system or another. Let people decide for themselves. Some people will immediately grasp the power of personal retirement accounts and their wealth-creating potential. Others will be wary. Still others will be bitterly opposed. That's OK! After all, we're Americans! Here, we are not told by the government whom to marry, where to live, which house to buy, what school to attend, or which movie to rent at Blockbuster over the weekend. Likewise, no one should be forced by the government to stay in the current Social Security system—or forced to use a personal retirement account—against their will.

The third fundamental principle should be **FISCAL ACCOUNTABILITY FOR TAXPAYERS.** Under no circumstances must we allow the Washington politicians to procrastinate or waste the Social Security surpluses. Instead, we need to impose fiscal accountability by using the hundreds of billions of dollars of mounting Social Security surpluses to help pay for a new system of personal retirement accounts for workers who want to participate in such a system. After all, very soon—by about 2015—those surpluses will dry up and be replaced by massive, mounting deficits. Washington will start paying out more in Social Security benefits than it receives in Social Security taxes. If we don't move quickly and decisively to reform this essential system—now, *before* it's too late—the fiscal crisis facing Social Security will hit us square in the face.

Today, there are a number of competing reform plans involving some version of Social Security Choice floating around in Washington, and surely there are more to come. As I've looked at the various plans, I've concluded that the following are the key elements that should be incorporated into a new system of Social Security Choice:

All workers under the age of fifty-five should be allowed to choose to stay in the current Social Security system, or invest a portion of their Social Security taxes in their own personal retirement account. Anyone older than fifty-five should be guaranteed the full benefits promised to them by the current system. Workers under fifty-five who choose to stay in the current system should be carefully informed by the Social Security Administration that the financial future of the current system does have real and serious risks (which I explain in more detail in the next chapter) and full future benefits cannot be guaranteed.

All workers who choose to use personal retirement accounts should be allowed to choose from a sensible range of safe investment options. These should include stock index funds, mutual funds, U.S. Treasury bonds, and other forms of safe, conservative bonds, and bank certificates of deposit—but not individual stocks, Asian derivatives, junk bonds, or other high-risk, speculative stocks (people can choose higher risk/higher yield investments in their non-Social Security retirement accounts, if they desire). All workers should be allowed to choose their own investment mix and change the mix as needed or desired. They should be allowed to choose a professional, qualified, and federally licensed, private sector financial services company through which to invest their money—and they should be allowed to change investment companies if desired. Sorry, no day trading.

All workers should be allowed to own their own personal retirement accounts—similar to 401(k) plans or IRAs—as their own private property. The government should not be allowed to own, manage, or take these accounts away.

All workers should have a financial statement sent to them quarterly explaining how their account is doing and how to make changes. They should also be allowed to access their account information on the Internet with a secure password and state-of-the-art privacy protections.

All workers should be allowed to choose a qualified financial planner to help them determine when to retire, how much money they'll need, and how to proceed. If someone wants to retire at age sixty instead of sixty-five, he or she should be professionally advised on how to do that. Likewise, if someone wants to retire at age seventy-five, they should receive professional advice regarding all the advantages, disadvantages, and various tax, Medicare, and other financial implications.

All workers should be free to leave the money in their accounts to the heir of their choice—including a husband, wife, and children. Also, this money should not be subject to federal taxes. It's not fair to impose a "death tax" on a grieving spouse and his or her children.

All workers should be required to use some of the money in their account to purchase private life insurance and disability insurance at low, competitive rates. To maintain the social insurance function of Social Security, workers should be required by law to buy adequate insurance to protect themselves and their families against disaster.

The federal government must guarantee all workers a minimum benefit—a financial safety net below which no one would be allowed to fall. Again, we must maintain the social insurance function of Social Security and reassure people that, while unlikely to be needed in a system of personal retirement accounts, the government will step in to help them if necessary.

There is, as you can probably imagine, plenty of disagreement—even among proponents of Social Security Choice—about how much money workers should be allowed to have deposited into their personal retirement accounts. Currently, the Social Security tax rate is 12.4 percent, half of which is paid by the employee and the other half of which is paid by the employer (those who are self-employed pay the full amount).

Some reform advocates suggest that a modest amount of, say, 2 percent be put into workers' accounts. The other 10.4 percent would go to pay current and future benefits and protect the social insurance function of the program (i.e., survivor's benefits and disability benefits). Others argue that workers should be able to put their entire half of the Social Security tax—6.2 percent—into personal retirement accounts and use their employers' half to cover transition and social insurance costs. Other major proposals would begin the program by allowing workers to have 4 percent of their income deposited into their own accounts and, over a period of time, phase it up to 8 percent, retaining the additional 4.4 percent to cover transition and social insurance costs. Still other proposals would eventually allow workers to put 10 percent or even the full 12.4 percent into their accounts.

What's the right answer? I'm not going to say. It isn't my aim to propose a detailed reform plan or settle this particular debate. I think you should decide and weigh in to your elected representatives accordingly. My goal is to persuade you and the politicians in Washington that we do need a new system started where workers can, if they want, choose to open their own personal retirement account. If Washington limits those accounts to only 2 percent of workers' income at first, that's OK, so long as we get started. Then, if a national consensus grows in favor of expanding the accounts, so be it. But whatever happens, let's not let the perfect become the enemy of the good. Too much is at stake.

In the next chapter, I'll show just how much is at stake—and just how much *all* Americans have to gain from Social Security

Choice. First, though, since a new approach to Social Security inevitably raises many questions, let me try to address some of those that are most frequently asked.

Q: *Would I be free to stay in the current Social Security system and not use a personal retirement account if I want?*
A: Absolutely. As I've already said, nobody's going to be forced to use personal retirement accounts. Everyone will be free to choose—that's the beauty of Social Security Choice.

Q: *Why not have the Social Security Administration get higher returns by investing in stocks rather than low-yielding government bonds?*
A: Absolutely not! A few years ago the Clinton-Gore Administration proposed such a scheme. But it's a terrible idea. It would allow the government to buy massive stakes in private enterprise and thus be able to control the direction of the U.S. private economy. This is not where we want to go. As humorist P. J. O'Rourke once wrote, "Having a government that owned economic assets is what made the USSR the success that it is today." Plus, politicians would inevitably come under pressure to invest in politically powerful businesses, politically correct businesses, failing businesses pleading for an infusion of capital, and all kinds of other businesses that may not be truly good financial investments. As Alan Greenspan, chairman of the U.S. Federal Reserve Board, has testified:

> Investing a portion of the Social Security trust fund assets in equities, as the [Clinton-Gore] administration and others have proposed, would arguably put at risk the efficiency of our capital markets and thus our economy. Even with Herculean efforts, I doubt

if it would be feasible to insulate, over the long run, the trust funds from political pressure—direct and indirect—to allocate capital to less than its most productive use.

Q: *If I choose to begin using a personal retirement account, what happens to the Social Security taxes I've been paying all these years?*
A: According to the most popular reform plans being discussed, you would still receive the portion of Social Security benefits in the future that you have earned based on the taxes you have already paid.

Q: *Do you advocate Social Security benefit cuts to "save" the system?*
A: No. Benefit cuts, tax increases, means-tested benefits, and raising the retirement age are all Washington's ways of betraying those who work hard and play by the rules. These solutions must be ruled out in definite terms and actively, vigorously resisted at every turn. Besides, as younger workers build up greater wealth in their own personal retirement accounts, benefit cuts won't be necessary.

Q: *I'm close to retirement now. Would it make sense for me to open a personal retirement account?*
A: If the politicians get their act together and pass legislation soon that allows you to keep fully all the benefits to which you're already entitled and allows you to put somewhere between 2 percent and 6 percent of your current income into a personal retirement account to be invested in the real American economy, then do it! These days, people are living ten, twenty, even thirty or more years beyond retirement. God willing, you will, too, and you will still need income just as the Social Security system runs out of money. So you need the higher returns from prudent, private

investment even *more* than anyone else will. And the sooner you are able to start such a private investment program, the better, even if you don't gain as much from it as a younger person who has a longer time to build up his or her account.

Q: *Would there be government regulation of private retirement accounts?*
A: There must be some basic, essential rules to protect workers' rights and uphold the highest standards of financial accountability and security. Obviously, we don't want the government to over-regulate and smother any new system. But the rules and regulations that currently guide the U.S. financial markets, the Securities and Exchange Commission, and the like work quite well. They can serve as a good model for a new system of Social Security Choice.

Q: *What about the administrative costs of having millions of personal retirement accounts?*
A: Experience with managing IRAs, and 401(k), and Keogh plans overwhelmingly suggests that administrative costs are a small fraction of investment returns. After all, technology continues to improve efficiency and competition continues to force down fees. William Shipman of State Street Bank estimates that the cost of administering a personal retirement account would be about one-fifth of 1 percent (twenty basis points in Wall Street lingo) of the account's value annually. Based on my experience, that seems like a pretty sound estimate.

More importantly, when people gain control over their retirement savings, they will be the ones to decide on the tradeoffs between the cost and value added by various investment managers. They will be free to pay higher administration costs if they think they are getting more for doing so.

Q: *What about all the people who don't have much financial experience or knowledge? How will they be able to run their own retirement accounts?*
A: First, the system would be designed to be easy for unsophisticated investors. They would be able to pick a major investment company from a list approved and regulated by the government, which would pick the investments for them. Countries that have already transitioned to an accounts-based pension system have found this mechanism to work quite well for lower income, unsophisticated investors who had little or no prior investment experience.

Second, as noted, there should be guidelines on what kinds of investment decisions people can make, so they can't go crazy and invest all their retirement savings in single stock tips overheard on the subway or in the checkout line at the grocery store.

Third, experience with IRAs, Keogh and 401(k) plans shows that individuals rarely try to make all the decisions themselves. They tend to rely on professional mutual fund managers, certified financial planners, and other advisors, as they should. This type of advice would be both permitted and encouraged for participants in the new system.

Fourth, a new system of Social Security Choice should be accompanied by a private and public sector educational campaign to help people better understand their personal finances and how the markets work. Let's help people help themselves by giving them the tools and information they need to make wise choices about their financial futures. Let's reintroduce classes into our public school system about how to manage one's personal finances and the importance of saving and investing. Many financial planners would gladly volunteer their time to teach local school children about finances and investments. This can only strengthen our society and give us an even brighter economic future.

Q: *I keep hearing about "transition costs." What are they and how will we pay for them?*

A: Transition costs are the amount of money needed to start funding personal retirement accounts for those workers who want them, while continuing to pay full benefits for current and imminent retirees, widows, orphans, the disabled, and other Americans entitled to Social Security.

The good news is that these transition costs will be paid for in several ways. First, according to Congressional Budget Office estimates (which have tended to *understate* the size of our surpluses), the phenomenal American economic boom is expected to generate $4.6 trillion in total federal budget surpluses during the next ten years. More than half of these surpluses ($2.4 trillion) would come from excess Social Security payroll tax revenues. This is because faster than anticipated economic growth has lifted tax revenues while relieving pressure on the federal government to spend money on welfare and other forms of poverty relief. We can begin using this money to shore up the current system and create personal retirement accounts for every worker who wants one. Never before in recent American history have we seen such potential for massive surpluses. It's absolutely critical that we put this money to good use—i.e., to finance a sensible, safe transition to Social Security Choice—before Washington finds new ways to squander all of our money.

Second, as individuals begin channeling more of their money into their own personal retirement accounts—and as this money is invested into productive American companies—this will provide a tremendous boost for our economy. A strong economy will, in turn, help generate still more tax revenue which can be used to fund the transition.

Third, individuals who wish to stay in Social Security will continue paying full payroll taxes into Social Security, and even individuals choosing to open a personal retirement account will continue paying a large percentage of their Social Security taxes into the current system. Thus, Social Security taxes will help finance the transition costs.

Fourth, the federal government could, if necessary, issue bonds to raise private capital. Nobel Laureates Milton Friedman and James M. Buchanan favor this approach because it would be an explicit recognition of future benefits owed to current taxpayers, debt we in effect already owe. I understand what they're driving at, and there's a definite logic to it. But I think in the current environment of massive budget surpluses, it may be unnecessary. Let's not take on more national debt—however temporary—if there's any way we can possibly avoid it. By wisely using the surpluses, I believe we can avoid any involvement with debt at all.

German ruler Otto von Bismarck introduced the first compulsory social security system way back in 1881. He defended it on the grounds that it made people dependent on the state: "Whoever has a pension for his old age is far more content and far easier to handle than one who has no such prospect." Bismarck *wanted* workers to feel this way. FDR definitely did *not* want this. Yet, the fact remains that Social Security has made countless Americans overly dependent on the government for their retirement security, while delivering a pitifully poor return on people's money. Is this the fair way to go into the 21st century?

Chapter Four

EIGHT REASONS WHY SOCIAL SECURITY CHOICE IS THE *FAIR* WAY TO GO

FAIRNESS. AS I SEEK TO PERSUADE YOU to support a new system of Social Security Choice and personal retirement accounts and that now is the best time to make the transition, many reasons come to mind. But the more I've thought about it, the more I've come to realize that the essential, fundamental reason we should embrace Social Security Choice comes down to the simple principle of fairness.

It's *fair* to revamp Social Security rather than let it collapse under the weight of promises that were made that can never be fully kept.

It's *fair* to refrain from imposing a massive, unfathomable debt— or a suffocating tax burden—on our children and grandchildren or from robbing benefits from those to whom they've been promised because we've been too lazy, distracted, or partisan to make sure the system is solvent.

It's *fair* to let the poor get richer along with the rich, which is exactly what happens when all people save and invest and get a superior return on their money, instead of forcing some people to live off their wages because they can't afford to save and invest.

Indeed, it's incredibly *fair* to let *all* Americans experience the magic of the markets and create substantial personal wealth. We shouldn't have to leave anyone behind.

But it is not necessary to force anyone to accept these views of what is fair. This is because the truly fair and compassionate thing to do is to give every worker the freedom to choose between entrusting his or her financial future to the current, government-run Social Security system or to a new, better system of personal retirement accounts invested in the private American economy. Here are the eight most important reasons why I believe that this is the case.

Reason #1: PERSONAL WEALTH CREATION
*Social Security Choice will help working families
create real personal wealth and retire with a nest egg
worth $1 million or more.*

After two decades in the world of financial planning—and after examining the various Social Security reform plans that have been developed in recent years—it is my conclusion that, yes, you really could wind up with a nest egg worth at least $1 million if you were free to choose the system of personal retirement accounts.

That's a pretty amazing claim, I realize. But the numbers really do work. Here's an example:

Let's take a newly married couple. The young man is, say, twenty-five years old and earns the median U.S. national income, about $32,000 a year. Let's say the wife works at home raising their children and does not make an outside income.

Now, let's assume that the young man receives cost of living increases over the course of his life but doesn't make huge leaps to higher levels of income.

Let's assume that like many young couples, this young couple has a difficult time saving and investing. They rarely have more than $1,000 in their personal savings account, and their company doesn't have a 401(k) plan or a pension plan. Unfortunately, they can't afford to put money into an individual retirement account.

But let's say that he and his wife choose to have 8 percent of their income deposited into their own personal retirement account each month. (That would be about two-thirds of the 12.4 percent Social Security tax; the other 4.4 percent would go to help pay the benefits of current retirees.)

Furthermore, let's say this couple chooses to invest in stock index mutual funds and receives an annual average rate of return of at least 6 percent, after discounting for inflation.

Guess what? Even without any other retirement income—from a public or private pension, a 401(k) plan, or an IRA—this couple could retire in 2040 with at least $1.2 million to their name.

At this point, working with an experienced, professional financial planner, they could develop a plan to draw down on this lump sum carefully and live off this money during retirement or buy a life insurance annuity that would pay them $100,000 a year (about $40,000 a year in today's money) until they pass away. Any way you slice it, even a couple earning a modest amount of money and having no other form of retirement savings or investments could live far better with a personal retirement account worth some $1.2 million than by entrusting their financial future to the overburdened and fundamentally unsound Social Security system.

Moreover, this example assumes a very young, single-earner couple earning a modest amount of money. Perhaps your situation is very different. Perhaps both you and your spouse work. Perhaps either or both of you make substantially more money than $32,000 a year. If so, you could easily build up *$2 million or more* in your personal retirement account, in addition to whatever other retirement savings and investments you have, ranging from a public or private pension to a 401(k) plan to various Individual Retirement Accounts you've already begun building.

The critical point to make here is that it's *your* money. Not the government's. Not the politicians'. Not the president's. It's yours. You worked hard for it. You earned it. And it's only fair that you get the best return you possibly can so that you'll eventually have enough to meet your financial goals and retire comfortably. That's what Social Security Choice is about, first and foremost: giving you the freedom to choose how your own money is invested so you get the best possible return.

As I mentioned earlier, the government-run Social Security system we have today gives American workers an absolutely dismal return on their money—less than 2 percent a year. That's the conclusion of a wide range of government and private sector studies and reports over the past two decades. President Clinton's 1994–1995 Social Security Advisory Council, for example, found that most American working families in the future will only be able to expect a 1 percent to 2 percent return on their money. A 1998 Cato Institute study found that the average, full-time, single worker will receive a mere 0.31 percent return on his or her Social Security taxes—and some will actually receive a return of negative 1 percent. In other words, workers will actually get back from the government *less* money than they put in over the course of their working years. It's unconscionable, but it's true.

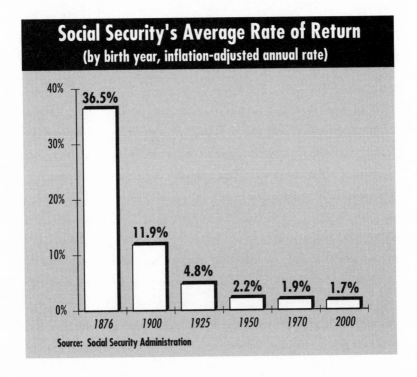

Social Security's Average Rate of Return
(by birth year, inflation-adjusted annual rate)

Birth Year	Rate
1876	36.5%
1900	11.9%
1925	4.8%
1950	2.2%
1970	1.9%
2000	1.7%

Source: Social Security Administration

Now, as far as I'm concerned, it doesn't matter whether you're liberal, conservative, moderate, Democrat, Republican, or Independent. We should all be able to agree that a 2 percent rate of return isn't fair for working families.

After all, you could put all your retirement savings in a federally insured savings account and get at least 3 percent interest every year.

You could get a 4 percent to 6 percent annual return on your money simply by buying super-safe U.S. Treasury bonds.

What's more, the average annual rate of return for U.S. stocks (measured by the S&P 500 index) for the 74 years between 1925 and 1999 was 7.0 percent per year.

In fact, what will you find if you go back over the past two hundred years? You'll find that U.S. stocks have averaged a 7.1 percent annual rate of return (adjusted for inflation and assuming the rein-vestment of the dividends). In fact, over the past two hundred years, the stock market has never lost money during any twenty year period. Not once. Never. Even the worst 20-year period, from 1929 through 1948—a period that saw the Crash of '29, the Great Depression, and World War II—still gave investors a 3.36 percent return on their money, better than Social Security provides today.

In the 1990s, of course, the markets have done exceptionally well, largely because of an explosion of innovative, new technolo-gies, lower global trade barriers, and a world largely at peace. As a result, it may be possible to average an 8 percent to 12 percent annual return simply by investing in good, safe, conservative mutu-al funds. And I'm not talking about betting the farm on high-fly-ing dot-com start-ups with twenty-something CEOs and roller coaster stock prices. I'm not talking about quitting your job and becoming an on-line day-trader, doing all your own market

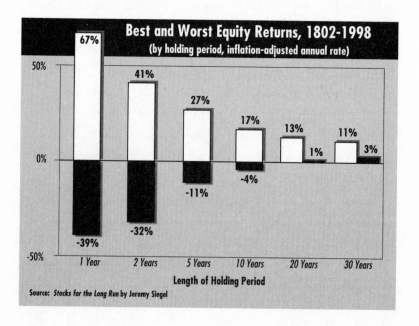

Best and Worst Equity Returns, 1802-1998
(by holding period, inflation-adjusted annual rate)

Length of Holding Period

Source: *Stocks for the Long Run* by Jeremy Siegel

research. I'm saying that just by buying a professionally managed mutual fund from a reputable financial services company that invests in a mix of profitable, prosperous, steady-growth companies, you could do four, maybe eight, possibly even ten times better than with the current Social Security system. So why exactly is it fair that the government should be able to make you settle for less?

Sure, the markets go up and down, but historically, they've mostly gone up. As Americans, we've suffered the Great Crash of 1929. We've suffered world wars, raging inflation, and numerous recessions. But over the long haul, nothing beats the performance of stocks. That's because the U.S. economy is healthy and resilient, and the value of stocks directly reflects the strength of the economy and the future earnings potential of a company. Despite numerous setbacks, the U.S. economy has grown spectacularly over time; thus, so have the value of American companies. Indeed, for the last twenty years we've witnessed the greatest bull market in human history. The Dow Jones Industrial Average of blue chip stocks has skyrocketed from about 800 in 1982 to upwards of 10,000 at the dawn of the twenty-first century.

As a result, even Americans who've invested just a little bit of money in the real American economy have seen their investments multiply in value again and again and again. They've gotten a tremendous rate of return on their money—far in excess of what the government delivers.

I've seen it firsthand. Americans have invested more than $30 billion through my company over the last decade because they want results. They want world class, highly trained financial professionals investing their money in the rapidly growing private economy. They want their retirement nest egg to grow—and grow fast. Faster than inflation. Faster than the rising tax burden. Faster than if they left their money in a savings account. Faster than their rising wages. Faster than if they tried to invest on their own in this rapidly changing, high-tech global economy. They also want security, peace of mind, and confidence. They want insurance against financial disaster. They want assurance of a better financial future. They want diversification—a prudent mix of financial vehicles to hedge against sudden downturns and reversals. So that's what our company provides. If we didn't, we'd be fired—and deservedly so.

Just look at the surge of new people investing their retirement savings in the markets in recent years. In 1980, for example, fewer than 6 percent of Americans owned mutual funds. By 1999 that number had climbed to 47.4 percent. Why? Again, it's not rocket science. Americans know that putting even a little bit of money into a mutual fund will allow them to get a far better return than

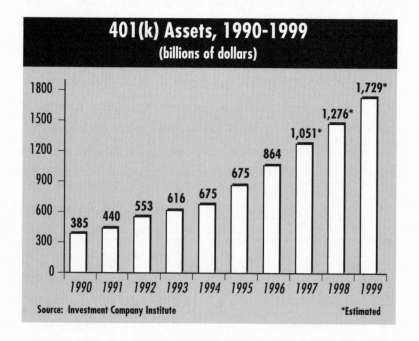

401(k) Assets, 1990-1999
(billions of dollars)

Year	Value
1990	385
1991	440
1992	553
1993	616
1994	675
1995	675
1996	864
1997	1,051*
1998	1,276*
1999	1,729*

Source: Investment Company Institute   *Estimated

relying on the government. The key now is to open the door to the other half of Americans who are being left out of this market-place miracle.

Reason #2: MORE SECURITY, LESS RISK
Social Security Choice offers Americans far more security and far less risk than the current Social Security system, which is financially unsound.

Wherever I travel in the United States these days, people come up and tell me they increasingly see depending on the current Social Security system as a greater risk than prudently investing in stocks, bonds, and mutual funds. It doesn't seem to matter where I am. It doesn't seem to matter with whom I'm speaking. It doesn't seem to matter what race or gender they are. Most Americans are worried about the future of Social Security. At the same time, they're also increasingly confident that the U.S. financial system is a far better way to create a safe and secure retirement package than depending on government—and, as I've explained thus far, they're right to be.

The battle raging between supporters and opponents of Social Security Choice and personal retirement accounts largely centers on the issue of *risk*, and understandably so. None of us can afford to gamble with our future. None of us can afford to be foolish or reckless.

The real question, then, is: Which do *you* believe is riskier—keeping your money in the current government-run Social Security system and trusting it to be there for you when you retire or putting part of your Social Security taxes in your own personal retirement account, invested in the private American economy?

Al Gore has long led the camp that says letting working families invest part of their Social Security taxes in the stock market is a "risky scheme," the equivalent of bungee-jumping off a 200–foot bridge with a 250–foot rope. He's not alone, of course. Hillary Rodham Clinton agrees with him, as do most leaders of the Democratic Party.

My view is the exact opposite. I'll talk more about where I think my party's leaders are going wrong in the next chapter. For now, suffice it to say that I believe the current government-run Social Security system was a pretty good deal for our parents and grandparents. Thus, I believe that we absolutely must keep the promises that were made to them. But as a Baby Boomer and financial services professional, I simply don't trust Social Security to keep its promises to me when I retire, and I don't believe you should either. Conversely, I believe the U.S. financial system has become so strong, so secure, and so well managed over the last several decades that it is far less risky to invest in mutual funds, IRAs, and 401(k) plans—and far less risky to create a new Social Security system of personal retirement accounts—than to depend on the government. My hunch is that you may feel this way also.

After all, as we've already discussed, a well-constructed Social Security Choice system would provide working families the ability to create real personal wealth by getting a far better return on their hard-earned tax dollars; provide a personal retirement account that they would own—not the government—which couldn't be taken away and wouldn't be taxed at retirement; provide low-cost, iron-clad private life insurance and disability insurance (with premiums paid from their personal retirement account); and provide assurance of a government-guaranteed minimum benefit, a monthly income below which no one—regardless of the state of the economy or the stock market—would be allowed to fall. That's real security in the real world—money you own, that you can see, that government can't play games with, *and* that government will supplement if all hell breaks loose.

Think of it like this. In the world of Social Security Choice, every worker holds his or her own cup. The government will make sure that no cup runs empty; investing in the real American economy will help make sure each cup overflows with abundance.

Perhaps Mr. Gore and I part company because of the different career paths we've chosen. He's spent his entire career in government. I've spent my career in the private sector. He has spent a lifetime taxing and spending other people's money. I've spent my lifetime helping people save and invest their own money. It has led us to different conclusions about the goals and aspirations of the American people and whether people have the intelligence and ingenuity to make their own choices and chart their own futures.

The interesting thing is that more and more Americans—particularly my fellow Baby Boomers—are coming around to my way of thinking. In fact, even some key Democrats in Congress have taken issue with Mr. Gore's point of view.

"Critics argue that individual accounts are too risky for lower-income individuals," wrote Rep. Charlie Stenholm, the Texas Democrat, in an essay in *Roll Call*, a Capitol Hill newspaper. "We believe that it is more risky, and certainly unfair, not to give lower-income individuals the opportunity to realize the benefits of accumulating assets. It is precisely this lack of investment opportunity that has left too many Americans on the fringe of the economy."

"Done in a correct way, individual accounts can be enormously progressive and very, very helpful, especially for low income workers in accumulating their share of the American dream," declared Sen. Bob Kerrey, the Nebraska Democrat, at a Washington press conference on May 4, 2000. "I think it's very important, especially for those of us who have already accumulated wealth, to try to write laws to enable other people to accumulate it and arrive where we are, as well. I think it's very important, especially for those of us who invested in the stock market, to be careful that we [not] say, gee, the stock market is too risky. Because we expose ourselves to the question, 'Well, Senator Kerrey, if you think it's too risky for the rest of the country, do you own any stock? Have you divested yourself of stock.... Are you relying only on Social Security? Is that what gives you a sense of security as you head towards the age of sixty-five?'"

"Democrats must stop perpetuating the myth that equity investment and the stock market are gambles only the rich can afford," wrote Sen. John Breaux, the Louisiana Democrat, in *The New Democrat* magazine (November/December 1998). "We must stop circulating horror stories about predatory investment advisers and market crashes. Doing so is misleading, counterproductive, and paternalistic. Yes, the stock market is risky. But experts agree that equity investment has a proper role in a long-term, prudent retirement strategy for individuals at every income level. Equity investment and the magic of compound interest should be available to every American. Without them, the poor and the near-poor will be pushed further to the fringe of the economy."

Let me share with you briefly why I believe the current Social Security system is far too big a risk to depend upon for the long haul.

Social Security has made $21.6 trillion in promises that can't be kept.

You think the $6 trillion national debt is a problem? You ain't seen nothin' yet! All throughout the twentieth century, the politicians in Washington made spectacular promises to young and old alike. They were promises that wouldn't need to be kept until the twenty-first century when—you guessed it—the politicians who made them would more than likely be dead and buried (having lived off million–dollar–plus congressional pensions during their "golden years").

Beginning around 2015, Social Security will begin to pay out more in benefits than it will take in through taxes. The annual deficits will mount up fast—$100 billion a year in 2021, $200 billion a year by 2026, and $300 billion a year by 2034.

Add up all those annual deficits—all those over-extended promises—between 2015 and 2075, and you wind up with a whopping deficit of at least *$21.6 trillion*, according to an analysis of the deficit projections contained in the Year 2000 annual report of the Social Security board of trustees. *That's almost four times the current national debt.* In my world, that's called an "unfunded liability"—and it spells trouble. Big trouble. The kind of trouble that sinks companies and makes shareholders flee for the hills. Worse still, the government is probably understating the magnitude of the problem. After all, the long-term deficit projection in the Year 2000 trustee's report was 7 percent more than their estimate in 1999, underscoring how difficult it is to measure the full magnitude of the problem we face over the next several decades.

One reason for these massive coming deficits is that Social Security was designed as a "pay-as-you-go" system. In other words, workers are taxed today to pay current retirees. The money you pay in Social Security taxes today doesn't really go to some account with your name on it (that's what personal retirement accounts would do). Instead, as you shovel the money in, the government shovels the money out.

That used to work just fine when there were forty or more

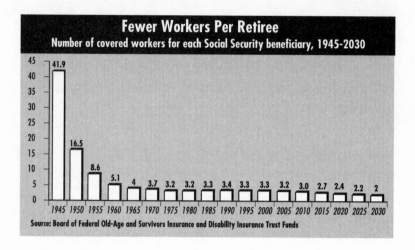

Fewer Workers Per Retiree
Number of covered workers for each Social Security beneficiary, 1945-2030

Source: Board of Federal Old-Age and Survivors Insurance and Disability Insurance Trust Funds

workers paying taxes to support every retiree. But the ratio of workers to retirees—that is, taxpayers to tax-receivers—has been plummeting in recent decades. Today, there are only about three people paying taxes to cover the benefit for every one Social Security beneficiary. Worse, with nearly eighty million Baby Boomers rapidly heading for retirement, it won't be long before there are only two people paying taxes to support every beneficiary.

Is it fair to make younger workers shoulder such an enormous burden if we could find an alternative, such as letting people save and invest through personal retirement accounts? No. I cannot bring myself to believe that it is.

Social Security gives you no ownership or firm legal claim to the money you pay into the system year after year.

Read that line again because it's hard to believe, I know. I wasn't sure I could believe it myself when I first read about this, shall we say, "little anomaly" in the law. But sure enough, as Social Security is currently set up, you and I don't have a contractual right to *any* specific future benefits. In other words, if you pay in $100,000 in Social Security taxes over your working lifetime, guess what? You don't have any legal basis to claim $100,000 in Social Security benefits, much less any more. You're at the mercy of whatever Washington decides to dish out in benefits when your turn comes around. Given the massive deficits coming over the horizon, you can expect to receive much less than you have paid in taxes (more on that in a few moments). Talk about unfair!

By contrast, if you were free to buy an annuity from a private life insurance company, you would know what benefits you would receive down the road and you would be legally assured of certain benefits. But not in Washington. There, the politicians can raid the so-called Social Security "Trust Fund," scoop out money to be used for all kinds of spending projects, toss in a few I.O.U.'s, and put off thinking about the size of your benefits until years later. And you have no legal recourse.

"I'd sue the government!" you say? "I'd take my case all the way to the Supreme Court!" Sorry, Charlie. Someone already tried to sue for benefits they expected but didn't receive from Social Security—and lost. The case, known as *Fleming* v. *Nestor*, was decided by the high court back in 1960. Listen to Justice John Harlan on the matter: "A person covered by the Social Security Act has not such a right in old-age benefit payment.... The non-contractual interest of an employee covered by the Act cannot be soundly analogized to that of the holder of an annuity, whose rights to benefits are based on his contractual premium payments...."

It gets worse: "To engraft upon the Social Security system a concept of 'accrued property rights,'" Harlan continued, "would deprive it of the flexibility and boldness in adjustment to ever-

changing conditions which it demands and which Congress probably had in mind when it expressly reserved the right to alter,
amend or repeal any provision of the [Social Security] Act."
Indeed, the "flexibility and boldness" to spend our money on
whatever the politicians choose. And this decision only confirmed
an earlier ruling, back in 1937, in which the Court declared, "The
proceeds of both the employee and employer taxes are to be paid
into the Treasury like any other internal revenue generally and are
not earmarked in any way." In other words, you and I are legally
obligated to pay into the system, but the government is not legally obligated to pay out.

The government actually effectively admits most of this in its
recent mailings to us about our Social Security accounts. You
probably got one of these recently. "In your Statement," the mail-
ing says, "you will see a year-by-year display of earnings that have
been reported to your Social Security record. You will also find
estimates of the benefits you and your family may be eligible for
now and in the future."

Notice the phrase "*may be eligible for.*" They don't say "*benefits
you have contracted for*" or "*benefits you are entitled to*" because if
Congress doesn't enact fundamental Social Security reforms, your
benefits are at risk of being cut. You don't *have* a contract for specific benefits, and you aren't legally entitled to them. The government's statement telling me what I "may be eligible for" is as
meaningless as the sweepstakes envelope from Ed McMahon
announcing that I may have already won $10 million.

The fair approach, therefore, is making sure a sizable portion of
your Social Security taxes are deposited in *your* own personal
retirement account that *you* own and that cannot be taken away
from *you*. After all, it's *your* money—not the government's.

Now, let me add a word here about the general sense of pessimism expressed by critics of Social Security Choice. I am sure many such critics come to their views sincerely. But I am dismayed by their unwillingness to trust the basic goodness, decency, and intelligence of the American people. They see Social Security Choice as a "risky scheme," and in doing so they seem to have an inordinate fear that life will go from good to bad and from bad to worse, the stock market will crash, the economy will plunge into the abyss, and tens of millions of Americans will be left in the streets and in the cold if we go to a new system of letting workers decide where and how to invest their own Social Security taxes. I believe those fears are woefully misplaced.

Yes, life has its ups and downs. But generally, over time, human beings make great progress. We make life better, not worse. That's been the history of the American people and nation. We've progressed from the bitter poverty of the Pilgrims and pioneers to the unprecedented prosperity of this present time. It hasn't been easy. Nothing good ever is. But our progress has been steady and substantial, and this should inspire us to have faith that the future will be even better if we make wise, prudent reforms now. After all, we know the current path we're on will bring real heartache and misery. So why stay on it? Why not make a commonsense course correction, knowing there are icebergs ahead?

One of the people who helped me come to understand these essential truths is a man by the name of Julian L. Simon, the late University of Maryland economics professor. In his lifetime, he carefully documented how the United States and global economies and the condition of human life at home and abroad have improved steadily and substantially over the long run. Back in the 1970s, in fact, Simon made a famous bet with Paul Ehrlich, a doom-and-gloom professor of economics who predicted that within twenty years the world would be engulfed in scarcity, famine, and misery. Simon fiercely disagreed with Ehrlich, believing that key resources like metals, minerals, oil and food would over two decades become cheaper, proof of their abundance rather than their scarcity. Simon won the bet.

"Let's begin with the all-important issue, life itself," Simon would go on to write in his book, *The State of Humanity* (1995). "The most important and amazing demographic fact—the greatest human achievement in history, in my view—is the decrease in the world's death rate.... The extraordinary decline in child mortality is an important element in increased life expectancy, for which every parent must give fervent thanks.... In the nineteenth century the planet Earth could sustain only one billion people. Ten thousand years ago, only four million could keep themselves alive. Now, more than five billion people are living longer and more healthily than ever before, on average. This increase in the world's population represents humanity's victory against death."

Food? "The long-run price of food is down sharply," Simon observed, "even relative to consumer products, due to increased productivity. And per-person food consumption is up over the last 30 years. The increased [average] height in the West is another mark of improved nutrition."

Education? Obvious problems aside, "consider the astounding increase since World War II in the amount of education that the youth of the world are acquiring," Simon noted. "This trend implies a vast increase in young people's opportunities to use their talents for their own and their families' benefits, and hence to the benefits of others in society as well."

Global unrest? Simon pointed out that while there will always be serious political problems, the world is clearly a better place since the Soviet Union and many other communist governments collapsed. Socialist governments everywhere have embraced free market reforms. Not only does this mean less warfare, it means dozens of countries are selling off poorly managed government enterprises. "It is the greatest sale in the history of the world," concurred authors Daniel Yergin and Joseph Stanislaw in their acclaimed book *The Commanding Heights*. "Governments are getting out of businesses by disposing of what amounts to trillions of dollars of assets. Everything is going—from steel plants, steel companies, and electric utilities to airlines and railroads to hotels, restaurants, and nightclubs. It is happening not only in the former Soviet Union, Eastern Europe, and China, but also in Western Europe, Asia, Latin America, and Africa—and in the United States, where federal, state, and city governments are turning many of their traditional activities over to the marketplace."

Global privatization means assets are going into the hands of private individuals who are free to manage them efficiently, increasingly free from political interference. Unlike central governments, which typically lost money on their nationalized enterprises, most of these privately owned assets will likely generate higher returns for investors. Higher returns means more capital to create growth and jobs, giving everybody a stronger stake in a peaceful world.

"People alive now," Simon concluded, "are living in the midst of what may be seen as the most extraordinary three or four centuries in human history," adding that "for most relevant economic matters, the aggregate trends are improving rather than deteriorating."

That said, why all the pessimism by the critics of Social Security Choice? Why all the fear that letting people save and invest a little bit of their own money will destroy all that is good and decent

Ida May Fuller of Ludlow, Vermont received the first Social Security check. Miss Fuller, a legal secretary, retired in 1940, having paid just $24.75 into Social Security during her working years. By the time she died at age 100, she had collected $22,889 in benefit payments. Social Security sure worked for her! But will it work for *you*?

in America? Again, such anxiety is badly misplaced.

Gambling is bad. But risk-taking in search of progress is good. Those who take smart, careful, calculated risks most often improve the quality of our lives. The real risk is *not* embracing careful, sensible change; the real risk is being paralyzed by fear and becoming stalwarts of the status quo. Again, it was FDR himself who told us, "The only thing we have to fear, is fear itself." Should we not heed his very words as we seek to improve his legacy?

Reason #3: A STRONGER ECONOMY

Social Security Choice will create a new pool of investment capital that will help the American economy grow stronger, creating new businesses and new jobs.

Picking up on Julian Simon's eternal optimism, it's hard to believe that just a few short years ago, no one had ever heard of the Internet. Only a handful of people had cellular or wireless phones. A personal computer filled an entire desktop, rather than fitting in the palm of your hand. Pagers were the province of doctors and firemen, not high school freshmen. Global positioning satellites were used to provide directional guidance to cruise missiles on their way to Baghdad, not to homemakers in minivans on their way to baseball practice. And doctors prescribed penicillin and vitamins, not Prozac and Viagra. But such are the times in which we live.

All around us we see dramatic new technological innovations that are revolutionizing how we live and how long we'll live. New tools are increasing our productivity, helping us work smarter, not harder. And greater productivity is helping us create an exciting, vibrant, dynamic New Economy that is consistently creating new jobs and new wealth.

The questions we must answer, of course, include:

- Will we continue to fan the flames of all this imagination and innovation and reach new heights, or will we let the coming Social Security crisis and its $21.6 trillion-plus mountain of debt derail this engine of progress and severely slow our growth?
- Will we allow every American to participate fully in this new era of prosperity, or will we hold hard and fast to the old rules that let the rich get richer and the poor get poorer?
- Will we reform government so it stops taking so much from workers and making their lives more difficult, and starts making peoples lives easier and gives workers more freedom, more opportunity, and more control over their money and their time?

From my vantage point, coming from the fast-growth world of financial services and retirement planning, one of the keys to future economic growth is avoiding the traps of massive tax increases and moving to a well-designed system of Social Security Choice. This would increase our national savings rate and create a huge new pool of private capital. This new fuel could then be invested into strong, successful, dynamic American companies, assuring that we can dramatically expand this period of prosperity, strengthen our country in a highly competitive global economy, and remarkably improve our quality of life. We can also help every worker become an owner, a stakeholder in this surging New Economy.

Americans are already becoming more comfortable with the power and promises of our financial markets. Over the past several decades, more and more people have begun to dip their toe in the Wall Street waters. Indeed, we're seeing the rise of a "New Investor Class." In the 1960s, for example, only 10 percent of Americans owned any stocks or bonds (directly or through mutual funds). Today, half of all Americans do. It's not just old, white, male, blue-blood, country clubbers creating wealth. Not even close.

- Some 55 percent of shareholders now are under fifty
- 47 percent are women
- Only 44 percent are white men
- Half don't have college degrees
- 35 percent are blue or white collar workers, rather than managers/professionals (29 percent)
- 10 percent are homemakers
- Minority participation is growing dramatically
- Half earn less than $50,000 a year and 85 percent earn less than $100,000 a year.

Clearly, a social and economic revolution is under way. We're witnessing the democratization of wealth. Main Street is joining forces with Wall Street. It's dramatic. It's historic. But it's not enough. The fact that half of all Americans now own at least some stocks and bonds is a good thing and a very good trend. But now we need to help the other half—the forgotten half—into a position where they can turn their wages into wealth, where they can experience the magic of the markets.

We also need to recognize the correlation between investing and innovation. The period in our history in which more and more Americans have begun investing in stocks and bonds has directly coincided with the period in our history when American entrepreneurs have stunned the world with new technological and medical breakthroughs. New capital has funded new ideas. New ideas have led to new companies. New companies have led to new jobs. New jobs have led to new buying power. New buying power has led to new sales. New sales have helped new companies grow. New growth has meant new value. New value has meant higher stock prices. Higher stock prices have meant new wealth for all investors, helping those with a little create a lot. And the Social Security Choice system I'm advocating will help us continue this powerful, prosperous cycle.

Indeed, Martin Feldstein—a Harvard professor of economics and president of the National Bureau of Economic Research—has studied the Social Security system very closely and concluded that moving to a system of personal retirement accounts would dramatically strengthen the U.S. economy, on the order of a $10 trillion to $20 trillion permanent addition to our GDP. (That's right, *trillion*—with a "t"!) In other words, rather than face an additional $21.6 trillion in oppressive national debt, we could experience upwards of $20 trillion in new jobs, businesses, wages, and savings. Indeed, this would mean at least one million new jobs, and $5,000 more income each year for the typical working family of four. No wonder Nobel Prize-winning economists like Gary Becker, James Buchanan, and Milton Friedman support moving to a new system of Social Security Choice and personal retirement accounts. It just makes sense.

Reason #4: LESS NATIONAL DEBT

Social Security Choice will help us pay down the national debt and get our nation's long-term finances back in order.

As we just saw, we have a choice between $21.6 trillion of new debt, or upwards of $20 trillion of new wealth. But let me take a moment to explain this a bit more clearly.

Every dollar that a worker chooses to put into a personal retirement account rather than leave in the current Social Security system is one dollar that is no longer a government liability. In other words, the government doesn't need to pay the dollar back as a benefit later on because that dollar is going to be invested into the private economy and grow at perhaps 6 percent or more each year. This is a big deal. Why? Because the government doesn't just take your dollar today and give you a dollar back when you're sixty-five. Inflation erodes the value of that dollar over thirty or forty years. So they're supposed to give you more just to let you break even. Then they are supposed to give you some kind of return on your money, even if it's a measly 1 percent to 2 percent. Again, this doesn't seem like a lot. But between inflation and even a low rate of return, the money the government will owe you three or four decades from now adds up pretty fast. So if people take their money out of the current system and the government is no longer obligated to multiply it over time to pay out even a meager benefit, then suddenly Social Security's $21.6 trillion unfunded liability begins to be erased very quickly.

Indeed, Gary and Aldona Robbins, economists who used to hold senior posts in the Treasury Department and have advised both Democrats and Republicans on Social Security reform, have concluded that a well-designed system of personal retirement accounts could completely erase that $21.6 trillion unfunded liability, assuming large numbers of people choose to use such accounts and are free to put a sizable portion of their Social Security taxes into such accounts. (This is a reasonable assumption if the experiences of other countries that have adopted Social Security Choice—we'll talk about them later—are anything to go by.)

But there's an additional advantage to Social Security Choice. If we do, in fact, create a vast new pool of investment capital to help fuel strong economic growth well into the twenty-first century, we have the real potential to reduce our existing national debt, not just eliminate potential future debt. Thus, not only could we prevent massive new tax burdens on our children, we may also be able to leave them a financial future free from the chains of our own making.

Now, you have to understand that the economists who work for the Social Security Administration are very cautious people. As they've developed their computer projections for the future fiscal health of this New Deal system, they've been very reluctant to expect the U.S. economy to be strong over the long haul. In some ways, you can't blame them. After all, most of them witnessed first-hand the economic stagnation of the 1970s and work for a government program developed during the Great Depression. So it should come as no surprise, I guess, that these are not a bunch of cockeyed optimists.

As a result, they have long projected the American economy in the twenty-first century to grow at no more than 2.1 percent to 2.5 percent a year. Recently, they modestly revised these estimates upward to between 2.8 percent and 3 percent per year. This is why they project such huge deficits—because, they believe, the U.S. economy simply won't be able to bear the enormous, mounting costs of Social Security as the Baby Boomers retire, given present tax and benefit rates.

But imagine, for a moment, that our economy grew at somewhere between 4 percent and 5 percent per year, after discounting for inflation. That may not seem like a big difference. But believe me, it's huge. In a $9 trillion annual economy, an extra point or two of economic growth means hundreds and hundreds of billions of dollars in added national wealth each year. That, in turn, would result in huge new levels of tax revenue. This money could be used to pay for the transition to the new Social Security Choice system and strengthen Medicare. Even then there would be money available to begin paying down our current $6 trillion national debt. And that's precisely what we should do. Is it really possible to grow at between 4 percent and 5 percent a year over the long haul? In this New Economy—a "new era of wealth," as economist Brian Wesbury puts it—it certainly is. After all, we've been growing at between 4 percent and 7 percent over the past several years, and this is just the beginning.

Reason #5: TAX FAIRNESS

Social Security Choice will help avoid the coming need for massive tax increases and benefit cuts, which would pit young people in a ferocious political battle against their parents and grandparents.

By letting all workers rapidly create real personal wealth in their own personal retirement accounts, this new system would eliminate the need for raising taxes and cutting benefits to pay for the coming $21.6 trillion Social Security shortfall. In turn, it would eliminate the bitter, caustic, and needless intergenerational battle that would undoubtedly ensue if young people suddenly saw their taxes skyrocket to pay for benefits for their elders that they knew they had little, if any, chance of ever collecting for themselves.

When government spends more than it takes in, it has several options. None of them are good. One of them is to raise taxes, which is what Washington has always done in the past when faced with Social Security shortfalls.

Do you realize that Washington has already raised the Social Security tax rate more than thirty times since the program began to keep it solvent—that's right, more than thirty times—from one percent in 1935 to 12.4 percent today! And that's just the tax *rate*. Of course, the amount of our income subject to Social Security taxes has also expanded dramatically. When the program first began, each worker's first $3,000 was taxed at 1 percent. Today, a worker's first $76,200 is taxed at 12.4 percent. That means that the maximum Social Security tax a person could owe has skyrocketed from $30 a year to $9,448.80 a year! Sure, most Americans don't make $76,200. But Social Security still punishes low- and middle-income workers making their way up the ladder of success. If they

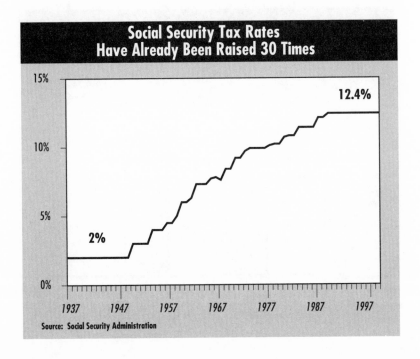

Social Security Tax Rates Have Already Been Raised 30 Times

Source: Social Security Administration

were getting a great return on their money, that would be one thing. But as we've seen, they're not.

As if this weren't bad enough, now the experts tell us that just to maintain current benefit levels for future retirees, the Social Security payroll tax rate will have to jump from 12.4 percent today to nearly 18.6 percent in the future—a 50 percent increase! Today, a working family earning $30,000 a year already pays $3,720 a year in Social Security taxes (12.4 percent of their income). How do you think they'd feel about paying another $1,860 a year? How would you feel?

Another real possibility is that Washington would remove the cap on Social Security taxes. That means all of a person's income would be subject to Social Security taxes, not just the first $76,200, as is currently the case. This would drive the top margin-

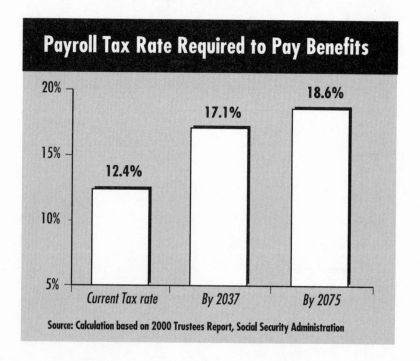

Payroll Tax Rate Required to Pay Benefits

Source: Calculation based on 2000 Trustees Report, Social Security Administration

al tax rate (the rate of tax paid on the next dollar of income earned) to 54.9 percent, the highest since the 1970s. Is this really fair? Do we really want tax rates as high as they were during a decade of high inflation, high unemployment, and stagnant economic growth? That's not exactly a prescription for prosperity.

The effect of such massive tax increases, however, would be more than universal anger among workers of all income brackets throughout the country. Were Social Security taxes to be raised on the order of 50 percent or more, the vibrant American economy would be severely hurt. We'd see slower growth, rising unemployment, rising business failures, distressed financial markets, and thus lower tax revenues—all of which would make it even harder (not easier) for government to keep its Social Security promises. To put it simply, we cannot save Social Security and strengthen America through massive tax increases. Yet those who oppose Social Security Choice and personal retirement accounts leave us with few other options.

Of course, there is another way government could wipe out such deficits without raising taxes: slash Social Security benefits to the bone. To make up for a $21 trillion-plus shortfall, experts have concluded that benefits would have to be cut by nearly one-third. That means Social Security checks—already miserly today— would have to be some 32 percent smaller in the future. How would you like to see your $900 monthly check chopped down to about $600 a month? Now, a one-third cut in benefits is bad enough on its face. But the reality would be far worse. After all, you have to factor in inflation, the skyrocketing cost of health care, and people living longer in the future and thus being retired for longer and needing *more*, not less, retirement savings. Any way you slice it, it's not a pretty picture.

That said, be on your guard! The folks in Washington may be dumb, but they're not stupid. They may very well try to use backdoor ways to trim benefits, such as raising the age at which you can start to receive Social Security benefits or imposing "means testing" so that those over a certain income can't collect as much (or any) of their benefits. These are also unfair and unwise policies, particularly when we have such a better alternative. But if we don't move to Social Security Choice, we can expect ideas like these to proliferate.

Personally, I don't believe that politicians in Washington will directly cut benefits, particularly by not to the great magnitude that would be needed to balance the books. After all, this would mean directly infuriating some eighty million Baby Boomers and risking harsh political retribution. Instead, I think it is far more likely that Washington will jack up taxes on Gen-Xers—and that's how the intergenerational war will get started.

President John F. Kennedy once vowed that America would "pay any price and bear any burden" to defend freedom against Communism. Surely, you and I would do the same to ensure that tens of millions of Americans aren't thrown into poverty upon reaching retirement. But must we pay such a high price and make our children bear such a heavy burden, if there is a better, more cost-effective way?

Reason #6: A FINANCIAL HEAD START FOR CHILDREN

Social Security Choice will allow workers to turn their wages into wealth and pass that wealth on to their children—tax-free.

"I look at my four children every day and realize the cliff that we're sending them over in terms of the Social Security system. What are we telling our children today? We're essentially telling them this: Here is a retirement insurance program for you. We take 12 percent of your income now and at least that much or more throughout your working lifetime, and we spend it. In exchange, you get at some future time—age 67 or possibly older—our promise to pay you an undefined rate of return. It may in fact be a negative rate of return. And you will get this money only if you live long enough to collect it. And when you die, your heirs will not get a cent. And, by the way, we can raise your level of contribution by any amount at any time. We ought to be able to do better for our children than that."

—REP. TIM PENNY, FORMER DEMOCRATIC CONGRESSMAN FROM MINNESOTA

Among the greatest features of a well-constructed Social Security Choice system is not only that workers are free to save and invest their own wages in personal retirement accounts and thus build up real personal wealth. Another great feature is that workers are also free to pass on their wealth to their spouse and to their children when they pass away. And they should be able to do so tax-free, without Uncle Sam getting another bite at the apple. That's why we need to make sure to eliminate the "death tax," also known as the "estate tax" or the "inheritance tax," as part of comprehensive Social Security reform. After all, it's not fair to tax assets that have been taxed multiple times before.

Think about it. What could be more fair than letting workers help their children get a financial head start in life by leaving to them a considerable sum of money with which they could pay for their education, pay off their debt, buy a first home, start a business, contribute to their church or synagogue or some other worthy charity, and/or continue to save and invest for their own retirement? What a wonderful gift for a parent to leave a child after years of hard work! And what could be more fair than letting parents pass on such assets tax-free, without upwards of 55 percent being seized by the Internal Revenue Service?

Consider a working couple with a personal retirement account worth upwards of $1.2 million to $2 million upon retirement. They could work with a financial planner to develop a strategy to draw down carefully on that money during their retirement years. At the same time, they could set aside a sizable portion of their lump sum and not touch it at all. This money could then be reinvested and allowed to grow in value over the five, ten, twenty, even thirty years of the couple's retirement. By the time the couple passes away, they could have an "estate" worth a considerable sum of money. Depending on how big of a chunk was set aside at the beginning, it is fully conceivable that even parents who earned a modest sum of money during their working lives could pass on an estate worth tens of thousands—even hundreds of thousands—of dollars to each of their children.

This stands in marked contrast to the current Social Security system. As things stand today, any benefits you don't "use up" before you die are, essentially, forfeited. They're not passed on to your children. The government keeps them. Is that fair? True, your spouse gets a modest benefit after you die, and that's a good thing, part of the social safety net we all want. But, believe me, such a benefit is nothing like the assets that could be passed down from a personal retirement account.

Consider, too, a couple that dies prematurely—before retirement. Under the current Social Security system, their children are eligible for a "survivor's benefit." This is good, too, part of the "New Deal" system of caring for those in need. But again, it's highly unlikely such a survivor's benefit would match the assets available to the children were their parents to have had their own personal retirement account(s). Isn't the fair and compassionate thing to make sure parents can pass as much money as possible on to their children when they die, especially if they do so before they even retire?

Reason #7: SOCIAL JUSTICE FOR WOMEN

Social Security Choice will end the injustice done to women—especially those who are single, divorced, or widowed—being left behind by the current system.

Another great feature of Social Security Choice is that it provides real social justice for women who have long felt left behind or discriminated against in their pursuit of financial independence and retirement security. Sure, Social Security provided an important degree of security for women throughout much of the twentieth century. But it also let women down in several key ways, as I'll point out below. And, compared directly to the value women can receive from personal retirement accounts, the current government retirement system falls woefully short.

Let's consider, for example, a real hardship case: a young, single mother—say, eighteen years old—struggling to make ends meet, providing for her child (or children) and carving out a future for herself. This young woman pays 12.4 percent of her already meager paycheck each week into Social Security. (Technically, she puts in 6.2 percent and her employer hands over the other 6.2 percent on her behalf, but it's all the same from her point of view.)

That's an enormous bite of a too-small apple, especially when you consider all the other bites that are taken (federal income taxes, Medicare/Medicaid taxes, state income taxes, property taxes, sales taxes, electricity taxes, water taxes, telephone taxes, and so on). Worse, what chance does she have of truly benefiting from this massive tax burden? Is she likely to get a comfortable retirement check way off around 2047, right when Social Security is going to be racking up unfathomable deficits? Hardly.

Now, if the government is going to ask a young, single mother to make such a financial sacrifice with each and every paycheck, it's only fair that the government make it worth her while. So, imagine that she could put a sizable portion of her income into her own personal retirement account. Imagine she were free to put up to, say, 8 percent of her wages (about two-thirds of the 12.4 percent of her wages that she pays into Social Security) into such an account, invested in, say, stock index funds, with an after-inflation rate of return of 6 percent a year. A stock index fund is a mutual fund that delivers a return similar to that of the overall performance of the market. If, for example, the S&P 500—the stocks of the largest 500 companies—delivers an overall return of, say, 10 percent, in a given year, then the return on a stock index fund would also be about 10 percent. Investing in such a fund helps a careful investor diversify risk and maximize gain by investing in many, many quality companies, not just a few.

In this scenario, in sharp contrast to the current Social Security system, this single mother could very well retire with upwards of $1.5 million to $2 million in her personal retirement account. Now she's turned her hard-earned low wages into real wealth. Plus, with the help of a skilled, professional financial planner, she could retire by carefully drawing down on her account and set aside a sizable portion for her children when she passes away. Or she could buy an annuity that would pay her upwards of $150,000 a year (or about $50,000 in today's dollars) until her death. Either way, this single mother would clearly do far, far better by saving and investing her money through a system of Social Security

Choice than by shoveling huge amounts of money into a system headed into an on-coming train. That's the power of personal retirement accounts.

On average, women tend to live longer than men, thus needing more retirement income. They tend to earn less than men, thus paying fewer Social Security taxes into the system. They often take years off from the workforce to raise children, thus putting no money into the system at all for long stretches at a time. They are more likely than men to work part-time, again meaning they pay less into Social Security. They are far less likely than men to have disposable income with which they can save and invest. They are far less likely than men to have a good pension plan—or any pension plan. For these and other reasons, women in the current Social Security system far too often find themselves at a serious disadvantage. Their benefits are lower than those of men. They can be thrown into poverty if their husband dies. Likewise, they can find themselves living in poverty—or at least far from comfortably—if they go into retirement single or divorced.

As a result, the rate of poverty among widows is 20.2 percent. That means that one-in-five such women are living in poverty. Worse, the poverty rate among single, separated, divorced, or never-married women over the age of sixty-five is a whopping 27.4 percent, or more than one-in-four such women living in poverty. All told, women over the age of sixty-five are nearly twice as likely to be living in poverty than men the same age. This is profoundly unfair and unjust.

Now, is this all Social Security's fault? Not entirely. The system was designed to supplement people's retirement income, not be a person's sole source of it. Nevertheless, non-married women rely on Social Security for about three out of every four dollars they need to live on upon reaching age sixty-five, and a large number of these non-married retired women depend on Social Security for 90 percent of their income. Given the chronic low returns they get on what little money they have paid into the system, many women are seriously financially hurt in their old age by the current system.

This is why a new system of Social Security Choice would be so much fairer to women. It gives all women—including those who are single, separated, divorced or widowed—the opportunity to retire with real personal wealth and be confident that the government will provide a guaranteed minimum benefit below which they will not be allowed to fall.

Reason #8: POVERTY REDUCTION
Social Security Choice will end poverty as we know it—particularly among African American and Hispanic families.

One of the most enduring legacies of helping workers to create real personal wealth would be simultaneously to help lift entire families, neighborhoods, and ethnic groups out of poverty, particularly chronic, generational poverty that is seen on so many city blocks and rural hollows in our country.

If moving to a new system of Social Security Choice means that even a minimum-wage earning family can retire with a personal retirement account worth hundreds of thousands of dollars— perhaps even $1 million or more if their investments do particularly well—just imagine how many Americans could be lifted into the middle class. Indeed, "middle class" may have to be redefined— upwards! Imagine, too, the amount of wealth that could be transferred to the children of poverty, giving them a dramatic financial head start in life. Making a transition to a well-constructed new system of Social Security Choice could turn out to be the biggest

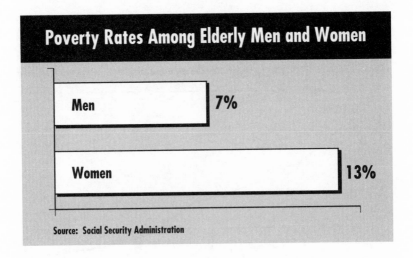

Poverty Rates Among Elderly Men and Women

Men — 7%

Women — 13%

Source: Social Security Administration

wealth-creating, poverty-reducing act in American history. Can you think of a more fair—and exciting—way to begin the twenty-first century?

Social Security was originally sold to the American people way back in 1935 as a policy for justice to provide a financial cushion so that people wouldn't have to suffer the hardships of poverty in their old age. Unfortunately, the current system isn't exactly working as advertised.

Among those hurt the worst by the current system are African American families, and particularly African American men who, on average, will never get back from Social Security what they have paid into it.

Tragically, many African American men die prematurely, before they reach retirement age. In fact, the median life expectancy for a black male born today is only 65.8 years. This means that half of all black men will *never* collect a single retirement check from Social Security! Moreover, since Social Security benefits aren't really passed on directly to wives and children (apart from a mod-

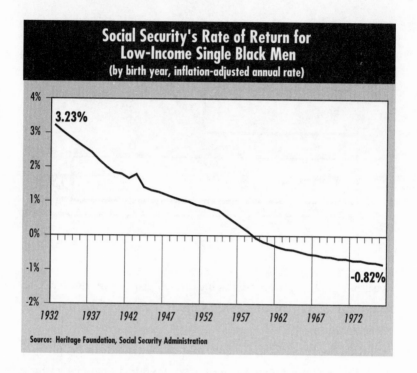

Social Security's Rate of Return for Low-Income Single Black Men
(by birth year, inflation-adjusted annual rate)

Source: Heritage Foundation, Social Security Administration

est spousal or survivor's benefit), many families never gain from their leading breadwinner's years of hard work and sacrifice. Where do much of an African American man's Social Security taxes go then? Incredibly, the system essentially transfers this money from blacks to whites, who, on average, get more education, start working and paying Social Security taxes later, and live longer to collect more Social Security benefits.

"What would be the public reaction if I proposed a plan to collect monthly contributions from working black men and women, then transferred a good portion of that money to older white women?" asks Robert Woodson, president of the National Center for Neighborhood Enterprise. "Or what would happen if I tried to sell a retirement investment plan to 24-year-old black American males that would end up paying each of them $13,400 less in benefits than they paid into my plan? Most likely, if I were successful in conning people into these schemes, I would be arrested, tried, and convicted of fraud. The troubling reality is that these are precisely the effects that today's Social Security system has on working class blacks."

"Is it fair to expect young black men to support a scheme that will not provide them with pension benefits until two years after they can expect to die?" asked syndicated columnist Deroy Murdock in an article in the *New Pittsburgh Courier*, a newspaper serving black readers. Obviously not.

Hispanic Americans are also terribly served by the current Social Security system. For example, "an average-income single Hispanic male born in 1975 who earned about $17,900 in wage, salary, and self-employment income in 1996 can expect to receive an annualized real rate of return from Social Security of just 1.44 percent," concluded Bill Beach, a Social Security expert, in a paper jointly published by the Hispanic Business Roundtable and the Heritage Foundation.

Hispanic *families* don't fare much better. "A Hispanic, double-income couple that has two children, that were born in 1965, and that earns the average wages received by Hispanic Americans can expect a rate of return of 2.17 percent from Social Security during their lifetime," concluded Beach. By contrast, Beach noted that if this couple were free to invest in a 50-50 stocks-and-bonds portfolio receiving, very conservatively, barely more than a 4 percent rate of return instead of a 2 percent return, they could easily retire with some $347,000 in their personal retirement account. Personally, I think a 6 percent rate of return or higher is more likely, allowing this family to retire with between $500,000 and $1

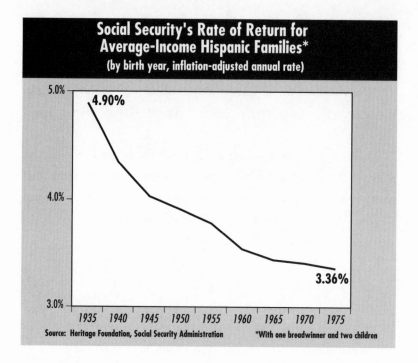

Social Security's Rate of Return for Average-Income Hispanic Families*
(by birth year, inflation-adjusted annual rate)

4.90%

3.36%

Source: Heritage Foundation, Social Security Administration   *With one breadwinner and two children

million. But either way, they'd still be far better off in a new system of Social Security Choice than being forced to stick with the current system, wouldn't you agree?

The bottom line is this: Why should working families living at, below, or anywhere near the poverty line be forced to pay for a lousy program, and be forced to accept pathetic returns? Why should anyone? We're not talking about being ripped off on a single purchase or maybe several years' worth of payments needed to buy a car. We're talking about payroll taxes taken out of the paycheck of working families for forty or fifty years, hurting most those who have the least! Is that fair? Not where I come from.

I believe every American, and particularly those who feel trapped by poverty, deserve a choice about whether to stick with such a system or to embrace a new system of wealth creation and poverty reduction. That's what Social Security Choice is all about.

Chapter Five

WHAT EVER HAPPENED TO THE
"PARTY OF THE PEOPLE"?

OK. WE'VE LOOKED AT what Social Security Choice is and why it's the fair way to save FDR's legacy and help people of every race, gender and income level create real wealth and financial independence. The real question now, of course, is: How do we turn all this rhetoric into reality? If personal retirement accounts are so great, how do we make sure every worker has the freedom to open one?

The answer, I'm afraid, leads us into the realm of politics. Either we pressure the folks in Washington to embrace Social Security Choice and begin making the transition immediately—while it can be done with relative ease—or we wait for the system to collapse, forcing us to fix it under less favorable circumstances. Unfortunately, the political class is, by and large, terrified of change. And they're not used to giving people *more* control over their own money; they're used to taking it away. So we're going to have to apply maximum pressure to get the job done.

But let me warn you in advance: Getting the politicians to wake up and smell the Starbucks won't be easy. Why? Because at this stage of the game, one political party gets it and one doesn't. And,

I confess, it's largely my party's leadership that stands in the way of real reform.

As I told you at the outset, I'm a Democrat. A Clinton Democrat. A Carter Democrat. An FDR-Truman-Kennedy-Johnson-Humphrey-McGovern Democrat.

You know all those Clinton-Gore campaign fundraisers—the ones that launched a thousand Republican allegations, investigations, and protestations? I go to them. I mix. I mingle. When I hear Newt Gingrich's name, I boo. When I hear Pat Robertson's name, I hiss. And then, when the appeal for money comes, I start writing my check. Not as much as the Chinese, perhaps, or those Buddhist monks, but I give. In the last decade, I've donated thousands of dollars to the Democratic National Committee and to the two Clinton-Gore campaigns. When Bill Clinton turned fifty, they

**The author with
the First Lady**

held a birthday party in his honor at Radio City Music Hall. They must have raised a fortune. I was there. In my office, I even have a photograph of Hillary and me. No kidding. I'm *that* kind of Democrat.

OK, I admit it: I haven't been thrilled by all the headlines the Clintons generated. Far from it. But if some minimum wage college kid at a phone bank in Utica, New York, called me at almost any point during the past eight years doing a national poll for some newspaper or TV network, I'd have been one of those Americans who "approved" of the president's job performance, who believed that the country has been basically on the "right track."

Why not? The economy has been fantastic since President Clinton took office in 1993. President George Herbert Walker Bush—Dad—took us into a recession. He wouldn't even admit it: "Not gonna do it. Wouldn't be prudent." (You can almost hear Dana Carvey saying it, can't you?) I mean, come on! The guy didn't know what to do when he broke his "no new taxes" pledge and the economy went south. He didn't know how to get us back on the right track; didn't even know what a grocery scanner was. He read off cue cards that said, "Message: I Care." No wonder he almost got his butt kicked by Pat Buchanan. For crying out loud!

But look at America now, eight years after the Clinton-Gore bus tour and "Putting People First." This isn't "stagflation," friend. You don't hear anything about "malaise" these days. In fact, for the past couple of years the economy has been cooking along at somewhere between 3 percent and 8 percent annual growth. Not bad, not bad at all. Inflation has plummeted. The stock market has skyrocketed. Unemployment is down. Trade is up. Poverty is down. Wealth is up. Crime is down. Small business creation is up. Everything that's supposed to be down is down, and everything that's supposed to be up is up. With Democrats at the helm. So there.

But let me tell you something. As a life-long Democrat, it pains me to say this, but I feel obligated to warn my party: When it comes to saving Social Security, building upon FDR's legacy, and helping working families create real wealth through personal retirement accounts, the leadership of the Democratic Party is dangerously out of touch with the American people. It's as though Al Gore is from Mars and Hillary Clinton's from Venus. They just don't get it. And if they don't start getting it fast, they're going to get left behind in a cloud of dust, with a mighty "Heigh ho, Silver, away!" echoing in their ears as millions of working families stampede to a political party that does get it, that promises to fight for their right to enter the New Investor Class and turn wages into wealth.

As I see it, the leadership of the Democratic Party is stricken with a historic case of Attention Demographics Disorder. They seem inexplicably inattentive to the financial aspirations of some eighty million Baby Boomers and forty-six million Gen-Xers who are America's future. Thus, as I write this in the summer of the year 2000, the Republican Party seems poised over the next several election cycles to reshape dramatically the political landscape. It's poised to transform itself from the "party of the rich" to the "party of people who want to become rich." Unless Democrats remake themselves quickly and once again embrace "bold, persistent experimentation," the New Republican Party could soon become home to tens of millions of working families, union members, single moms, African Americans, and Hispanics who want to participate in this incredible era of prosperity. These are Americans who want to retire as millionaires, who believe in the Gospel According to Regis, and who absolutely—and justifiably—refuse to be left behind during the greatest era of wealth creation in the history of the world, and we must fight hard to retain their loyalty.

Just as a generation of working class social conservatives fled from the Democratic Party to the Republican Party in the 1970s and 1980s, I believe that a new generation of savings and investment-minded *fiscal* conservatives—"New Democrats" who are part of the emerging "New Investor Class" or who eagerly want to become part of the "New Investor Class"—are now also poised to flee to the GOP. Why? Because after much internal debate and division, the leadership of the GOP has decided to embrace the future and champion Social Security Choice. Indeed, the story of how such an epiphany happened is quite instructive.

On September 22, 1995, a man with no elected political experience stood before a throng of reporters and camera crews at the National Press Club in Washington, D.C., and declared himself a Republican candidate for president of the United States. A mere asterisk in the polls, he would go on to describe himself as an "entrepreneur," an "outsider," and a "risk-taker," someone who would "unlock the stranglehold that the political class has on American life." He vowed to offer sweeping new ideas to give working families more control over their money and their retirement savings—from a "flat tax that's a tax cut" to "a new Social Security system for younger workers." His name was Steve Forbes, then forty-eight, editor-in-chief of one of the world's leading business magazines, and president and CEO of Forbes, Inc., his family's publishing empire. The snickering among the political professionals began immediately. No one—I confess, not even I— foresaw the impact this unlikeliest of candidates would have on the national debate, particularly with regard to Social Security Choice.

Indeed, when Forbes first got into the 1996 presidential campaign, he struck me as someone who must have been invented by
the opposition research department at the Democratic National
Committee. I had a mental image of a bunch of grizzled, liberal,
political operatives—hair a bit tousled, ties askew, sitting in a win-
dowless basement war room (not smoking, of course—they're
Democrats!)—brainstorming and taking notes on a white board
mounted on an easel, rubbing their hands with glee, building their
"dream" Republican candidate: a white, Wall Street gazillionaire
with his own private plane, helicopter, yacht, Moroccan palace, and
Fiji Island; someone straight out of Democratic central casting. But
Forbes refused to be typecast. Indeed, he was a man on a mission.
Yes, he was a political outsider, but he was hell-bent on forcing his
party's insiders to court and capture the New Investor Class. Yes,
he was wealthy, but he alone among the presidential candidates of
either party was offering sweeping new ideas to help working
families get wealthy, too. "I'm like an entrepreneur with a new
product," Forbes would say to reporters, confident he had a winning message on his hands. "Not until you actually put it in the
marketplace will you find out if it actually works."

Forbes has a great passion for the Social Security issue, long
known as the "third rail of American politics." His eagerness to
seize this issue with both hands caught my attention. After years in
the world of financial services and retirement planning, I, too, had
been coming to a similar conclusion during the early 1990s: that
a 401(k)-like approach to Social Security was the best and fairest
way to go. But I'm not sure I expected someone to have the political *cajones* to lead the way so soon.

For some time, I'd been reading the writings of Pete Peterson,
an advisor to several U.S. presidents, a former commerce secretary,

and an investment banker. Peterson had long been warning of the impending collapse of Social Security due to the coming wave of retiring Boomers. In fact, in October of 1996, Peterson published a book that had a great impact on my thinking, entitled, *Will America Grow Up Before It Grows Old?: How the Coming Social Security Crisis Threatens You, Your Family, and Your Country*. I also had been struck by a September 1994 survey conducted for Third Millennium, a group of Generation X activists. It found that more young people believe in UFOs (46%) than believe that Social Security will be there for them when they retire (28%).

At the same time, I was also paying quite a bit of attention to various proponents of an IRA/401(k)-like solution to Social Security. In 1994, for example, I had invited a young economic policy expert named Steve Moore from a libertarian think tank in Washington, D.C., called the Cato Institute, to speak at a conference on retirement planning and investing that my company was sponsoring. He and some of his colleagues in Washington had for years been making the case for a new Social Security system of personal retirement accounts. Now—suddenly and unexpectedly, in the fall of 1995—such ideas were garnering national attention.

You might have thought at the time that all Republican candidates would embrace helping middle-class workers invest in the stock market—but you would have been dead wrong. Almost in unison, the GOP hierarchy fiercely resisted the idea and sought to destroy Forbes for bringing it up at all. After all, the GOP had been badly burned by the Social Security issue back in 1964 when Barry Goldwater spoke of "privatization" and lost disastrously to Lyndon Johnson, and again in 1986 when Senate Republicans tried merely to discuss entitlement reform and in turn lost control of the Senate. So Sen. Bob Dole, the eventual GOP presidential nominee, and his political operatives pummeled Forbes and his Social Security ideas as "risky" and "untested." Nelson Warfield, Sen. Dole's press secretary, let loose with lines like, "Mr. Forbes' idea of hardship is when the butler has a day off, so he's willing to toy with risky schemes like privatizing Social Security so many depend on." A stinging Dole TV ad was whipped up that declared, ominously: "Steve Forbes plans to end Social Security as we know it." Yet despite attacks like these, Forbes's ideas gained popularity.

Even more unbelievable was that the news media—in nearly all ways hostile and dismissive of Forbes (and particularly of his flat tax)—actually found Forbes's new Social Security ideas intriguing, even gutsy. *Newsweek* columnist Joe Klein, for example, wrote that Forbes "has been especially courageous in telling the truth about Social Security, proposing a gradual transition to the sort of privatized, though mandatory, system that was pioneered in Chile and is now being adopted in many developing countries."

Ultimately, the unified attacks on Forbes at the hands of his fellow Republicans took their toll. But by the time Forbes bowed out of the 1996 campaign, even Sen. Dole was backing off his harshest attacks, conceding that personal retirement accounts might, in fact, merit a second look. Congressional Republicans began quietly considering legislation to create personal retirement accounts. And I began hearing more and more rumblings that senior Democrats—even President Clinton and his top advisors—were taking a closer look at the idea. A new flurry of articles and editorials and grassroots efforts devoted to promoting such accounts could be seen popping up all across the country.

With all the positive attention toward personal retirement accounts, of course, came the inevitable critiques and counterattacks. This included cover stories in liberal, intellectual magazines such as:

"Uh-Oh: Social Security Is on the Skids;
Does Anyone Over Forty Give a Damn?"
—*The New Republic*, April 15, 1996

"Up in Smoke: With Billions at Stake, Wall Street
Is Quietly Lobbying to Privatize Social Security in 1997;
Both Parties—and the President—Are Listening"
—*Mother Jones*, December 1996

"Social Insecurity: The Campaign to Take the System Private"
—*The Nation*, January 25, 1997

But by this point, the idea of personal retirement accounts had entered the political bloodstream. It was rapidly gaining popular support. It was not easily stopped, and its opponents had no ready, effective antidote. Indeed, before such opponents fully realized what was happening and could develop a plan of attack, a new poll was taken by Mark Penn, the president's own pollster, for the Democratic Leadership Council (DLC). The results, released in December of 1996, were stunning.

Question: Do you think it would be better to stay within the existing system—for example, raise payroll taxes and cut benefits—or would it be better to move toward more structural changes to Social Security like letting people control portions of their own retirement savings?

- 67 percent of Americans said it would be better to "move toward more structural changes" and "let people control portions of their own retirement savings."
- Only 25 percent of Americans said they preferred to "stay within the current system" and "raise payroll taxes and cut benefits."

Incredible. According to President Clinton's own pollster, a "fringe" idea almost universally considered political kryptonite in December of 1995 was supported by upwards of two-thirds of the American people in December of 1996, only one year later. Nor was the DLC poll an anomaly. It mirrored a poll taken in August of 1996 by a firm called Public Opinion Strategies which found that 69 percent of Americans favored the option of "allowing individuals to invest their payroll taxes in an IRA-type account," while only 12 percent opposed this idea. Meanwhile, grassroots groups of all ideological stripes began educating people about Social Security Choice and organizing and mobilizing support for the program.

The Clinton-Gore administration missed the chance to use FDR's "bold, persistent experimentation" to save Social Security.

By January of 1997 the Clinton-Gore administration's Social Security Advisory Panel unanimously agreed that investment in the stock market could provide a greater return for workers and their families than the current Social Security system, and a majority of the panelists (seven out of thirteen members) favored some form of individual control of Social Security investments. Coming from a group appointed by a Democratic president, one enamored of FDR's legacy, it was a remarkable event.

By his State of the Union address in January of 1998, President Clinton was calling for bipartisan consensus in the battle to "save Social Security." Rumor had it that the White House was seriously considering embracing a form of personal retirement accounts, at least until the Clinton-Lewinsky scandal exploded onto the headlines and derailed the administration's entire legislative agenda.

By the spring of 1999 Forbes was again running for president. He again ran millions of dollars of TV and radio ads advancing his ideas. He again challenged the GOP establishment to embrace Social Security Choice fully and completely. And this time his challenge to the GOP front-runner, Texas Governor George W. Bush, from the right side of the political spectrum, was matched by a powerful challenge from the left in the person of Sen. John McCain of Arizona. Since 1996, Senator McCain had also become a strong supporter of personal retirement accounts, and together, Forbes and McCain tag-teamed Governor Bush into not only embracing the rhetoric of Social Security Choice but actually making it a major element of his 2000 presidential campaign.

The pincer movement worked. In 1997, Governor Bush had privately told Social Security reform experts from the Cato Institute that while he was intrigued by the idea of personal retirement accounts, there was, essentially, no way in hell that he could touch the issue publicly if he had any chance to win the presidency. Too much political pain for too little gain. Yet by the time the Republican presidential primaries were over three years later, Governor Bush and his allies in the GOP establishment were fully and completely on board.

In May of 2000, Governor Bush made Social Security Choice and personal retirement accounts the centerpiece of his presidential campaign against Vice President Al Gore. "Personal accounts build on the promise of Social Security—they strengthen it, making it more valuable for young workers," the Texas Governor said in a major speech to a group of retirees at the Rancho Cucamonga Senior Center in California. "Senator [Daniel Patrick] Moynihan, a Democrat, says that personal accounts take the system to its 'logical completion.' They give people the security of ownership. They allow even low-income workers to build wealth, which they will use for their own retirement and pass on to their children."

In his speech, Governor Bush outlined the six principles he had chosen to embrace to guide his approach toward Social Security reform:

- Modernization must not change existing benefits for retirees or near-retirees
- The Social Security surplus must be locked away only for Social Security
- Social Security payroll taxes must not be increased
- The government must not invest Social Security funds in the stock market
- Modernization must preserve the disability and survivors components
- Modernization must include individually controlled, voluntary personal retirement accounts, which will augment the Social Security safety net. These accounts will earn higher rates of return, have parameters of safety and soundness, and help workers build wealth that can be passed on to their children.

It was a bold, unexpected move, remarkable for a man then better known for his personal charisma than his political imagination, and the son of a former president who had broken faith with the emerging New Investor Class by breaking his "no new taxes" pledge and leading the country into a recession.

It caught people's attention. Especially Vice President Gore's attention. Gore immediately attacked personal retirement accounts as a "secret," high-risk gamble. "You shouldn't have to roll the dice with your basic retirement security," he told reporters. A Gore 2000 press release issued the same day as Governor Bush's speech warned that under Bush's plan, "individuals could lose some or all their invested money, threatening the basic Social Security guarantee for future retirees." The release added that "the natural fluctuations in the stock market could force massive government bailouts of Social Security during market downturns or for people who make poor investment choices" and that "$1 trillion [in] privatization transition costs" could leave the nation with "trillions of dollars of debt."

Yet this blistering and disingenuous attack came from a Vice President who had simultaneously presided over one of the greatest bull markets in American history *and* a do-nothing approach to saving Social Security. Yes, the Clinton-Gore Administration had talked for nearly three years of pursuing a bipartisan solution to the Social Security crisis. But it had done nothing to solve the crisis. When it came to offering a positive, forward-looking solution, the White House seemed to have nothing constructive to say. In one of the great shames in the history of the party of FDR, it became the Republicans who were alone in proposing innovative solutions and Big Ideas. The White House couldn't seem to find its voice.

Worse, in the spring of 2000, Vice President Gore decided to utterly flip-flop on the need to "save Social Security" and said with a straight face, "If it ain't broke, don't fix it."

Why are Al Gore (shown here with Congressman Gephardt, left) and other Democratic leaders so out of touch with the true priorities of the American people?

"Ain't broke"? Is that like, "I invented the Internet"? Is that like saying he and Tipper were the inspiration for *Love Story*? Good grief! How could a sitting Vice President – blessed with access to the best of modern political polling – be so out of touch with reality and the sentiments of the American people?

According to a May 1999 poll jointly conducted by National Public Radio, the Kaiser Family Foundation, and the Kennedy School of Government (not exactly a troika of right-wing conservatives):

- Only 23 percent of Americans believed "Social Security is basically working well as is, and Congress should continue to make only gradual adjustments to preserve the program for future generations." In other words, only 1 in 4 Americans took Mr. Gore's position.
- A stunning 75 percent of Americans said "we need to make major changes to Social Security soon, to keep the program from running out of money when the Baby Boom generation retires."

In other words, people got it. What's more, growing numbers of Americans know *why* the system is in trouble:

- 58 percent of Americans believe a major reason Social Security faces financial difficulties is because "more people are going on Social Security and there will be fewer workers to pay Social Security taxes to support them."

■ 53 percent believe a major reason is that "people on Social Security are living longer so they cost the program more money."

■ 65 percent believe a major reason is that "money in the Social Security Trust Fund is being spent on programs other than Social Security."

Even more fascinating is that large numbers of Americans have strong feelings about what *not* to do to save Social Security:

■ 90 percent oppose "reducing Social Security benefits," and of that number, 73 percent "strongly" oppose reducing benefits.

■ 67 percent oppose "gradually raising the retirement age for Social Security to age 70 over the next 20 years."

■ 63 percent oppose "raising the amount of taxes higher-income retirees pay on their Social Security benefits."

■ 61 percent oppose "increasing the amount employers and employees pay in taxes to Social Security."

Now, the most interesting number of all:

■ 65 percent of Americans polled by National Public Radio, the Kaiser Family Foundation, and the Kennedy School of Government said they favored "people having individual accounts and making their own investments with a portion of their Social Security payments." Remarkable, especially considering the generally acknowledged liberal leanings of the organizations sponsoring and conducting the survey.

With such powerful, compelling evidence, why did Vice President Gore dig in his heels against a reform idea so popular with Baby Boomers and Gen-Xers, an idea a Democratic president should champion, not chew up and spit out? I suspect it was one part habit—Democrats had *always* opposed such ideas—and one part political calculation. The liberal leadership and left-wing allies of my party have always preferred welfare over wealth creation and anti-Wall Street populism to New Investor Class pragmatism, and the Vice President desperately wanted to energize his more liberal base.

By June, however, the Vice President had discovered that his attacks weren't working as planned. He was losing ground to Governor Bush on the Social Security issue and he needed to chart a new course. So almost one month to the day after Governor Bush's Social Security speech, Vice President Gore unveiled his "Retirement Savings Plus" plan.

According to a Gore 2000 fact sheet, the plan would "create tax-free savings accounts" in which the federal government would "match individual contributions with tax credits, with the hardest-pressed working families getting the largest tax credits." Thus, each spouse could contribute $500 to his or her account and would receive a three-to-one matching grant, or $1,500, providing a total annual account of $2,000. Over the course of thirty-five years, the Gore campaign stated, a couple making less than $30,000 could build up a nest egg of more than $400,000. But the Vice President adamantly (and preposterously) insisted this was in no way, shape or form, similar to the personal retirement accounts proposed by others. Yeah, right.

"I have always supported private savings and investment, and I've always supported additional incentives for middle-income and low-middle-income families to save and invest more," the Vice President declared. "But I have never supported plans that would steer the money you pay into Social Security into the stock market. That would undermine America's trust in the trust fund, and take the 'security' out of Social Security."

Sadly, the proposal was insincere because it promised to "save Social Security" while doing absolutely nothing to shore up the system's $21.6 trillion-plus unfunded liability. Nor would it protect Baby Boomers and their children from a coming 50% payroll tax increase and/or a one-third cut in benefits. On top of all this, in order to qualify for the Gore proposal's matching funds, poor families already living on the edge would be required to scrape up even *more* money each month to put into these new accounts. How is this fair? Wouldn't it be better to let families put part of the money they're *already* paying into Social Security into a personal account that gets higher returns?

The proposal was hypocritical because it was based on a premise that Al Gore has been forever and ferociously attacking—the value of saving and investing in the U.S. stock market. How can someone bitterly attack as a "risky scheme" and a foolish "roll of the dice" a plan to allow families to save and invest some of their own money in stocks and bonds for their own retirement if he is simultaneously proposing a variation of such a plan, however flawed? Either the stock market is a terrible place to invest for the future, or it isn't. Either Wall Street's trying to rip off Main Street, or it isn't. You can't have it both ways.

I had dinner with then-Senator Gore back in 1987. It was early on in the pre-presidential primary season, and a friend of mine was running Senator Gore's Florida campaign. At the time, I was actually supporting Gary Hart, the New Democrat-style Bill Clinton of his day (in more ways than one, I guess). Anyway, I remember my friend wanting me to meet this up-and-coming senator from the South. So I did. Since then, I've heard a lot of people say how warm, personable, and sincere Al Gore can be in intimate settings, or behind closed doors. I saw elements of this that night, but I remember also seeing the kinds of elements Jay Leno likes to pick on in his monologues.

The point is, despite presiding over the greatest bull market in history, Al Gore and the Democratic party are missing a golden opportunity to appeal to the dreams and aspirations of the New Investor Class—the tens of millions of Americans who own their own homes, own at least a few stocks and bonds, are getting hooked up to the Internet, and are learning the new rules of the New Economy. The reality is that the American people can no longer be well understood through the lens of ideology. We are a country of pragmatists, and an exponentially growing percentage of Americans have been entrusting their long-term wealth to ownership in the basic industrial fabric of our nation—stocks, bonds, mutual funds, variable annuities. People's general experience with 401(k)s, IRAs, 403(b)s, SEPs, SIMPLEs and other defined contribution vehicles has been overwhelmingly positive. They are amazed at the growth of their savings over the last decade and a half, and they are comfortable with the concept of self-directed investing.

Then there are the dreams and aspirations of the rest of the American workforce—those who want to participate in this age of prosperity but feel left behind, those who aren't wired but want to be, those who aren't yet wealthy but could be and should be well on their way. All of these men and women increasingly recognize that we live in an incredible age of progress, where change is no longer the side dish of our times, it's the main course; not the spinach, but the steak.

Sure, if you'd asked a vast majority of Democrats thirty years ago, there's no question they would have said it was far more risky to invest a person's retirement savings in stocks and bonds than to trust Social Security. My family would most certainly have been among them. When I became a teenager in 1973, for example, America was embroiled in the Vietnam War. The Cold War was colder than ever. The Soviets were our mortal enemies, trying to take over the world. The Arabs were trying to wipe out Israel and prohibiting us from buying their oil. Inflation was rising. The economy was slowing. The stock market was stagnant. Watergate was becoming a household word. Some of you remember it well.

But that was then. The Soviet Union has since ceased to exist, the Cold War is over, and the United States is now the world's only military superpower. Free elections and free speech are sweeping the globe, and peace is breaking out in the most unlikely places. The Digital Age is changing everything, giving all of us more control over our lives, and the United States is also now the world's only economic superpower. Free markets and free trade are sweeping the globe, and breathtaking new technologies arrive almost daily. Today, everything is different than when we grew up.

War is out—wealth is in.
The Berlin Wall is out—Wall Street is in.
Barbed wire fences are out—wireless phones are in.
Nuclear stockpiles are out—the New York Stock Exchange is in.
The Russian Bear is out—the Merrill Lynch Bull is in.
Mutual Assured Destruction is out—mutual funds are in.
The commies are out—dot-coms are in.
NATO is out—NASDAQ is in.
The IRA is out—IRAs are in.
The KGB is out—401(k)s are in.
The CIA is out—CNBC is in.

Today we live in a whole new world. It's time to adapt. I have.

You have. But too many leaders in my party have not.

Don't get me wrong. I understand the world to which they're clinging. I understand it all too well. My parents, Adrian and June Dokken, were old-line Democrats. *Their* parents were old-line Democrats. And their parents were the pilgrims of progressivism, who immigrated to America from Norway in 1881 and wanted to create a better, fairer, safer, saner world for their children. They homesteaded in a tiny little village called Towner, North Dakota, in the Sand Hills of McHenry County. "Tiny" barely does it justice. We even had the proverbial one-room schoolhouse, and all the kids were Democrats because all the parents were Democrats. Well, almost all. There were a few Republicans. Out of fifty-four votes on the local township committee, maybe six were Republicans. If some issue ever garnered seven Republican votes, the town was abuzz: "Who's the turncoat? See if *he* gets his road plowed this winter!" And where I come from, not getting your road plowed for an entire winter was a serious problem.

As a young boy, I was an active member in the Farmers Union, an agricultural cooperative, attending its summer camp for kids and learning to be a dyed-in-the-wool John Steinbeck socialist. Hell, we were practically communists—and we loved every minute of it! When I was eight, I went door-to-door, passing out leaflets, stumping for Vice President Hubert Humphrey for president.

Every week when I was young, a friend of my family's let me read his copy of the *New Republic*, the liberal Democratic news and issues magazine, and I devoured each and every word. When I was done, I'd devour *Time* magazine, for which I had my own subscription, paid for with my allowance money. I just didn't want to be out of the loop. From the age of eight on, I don't recall ever thinking that I wanted to do anything else but be in public service and run for public office—as a Democrat, of course. For me, there wasn't any question. Mine was the party of the people, the party of Main Street. Theirs was the party of big business, the party of Wall Street. I wanted to fight for the little guy, and I was completely focused on my little life mission. In high school I remember helping Lloyd Omdahl, a former Democratic lieutenant governor, run for Congress. Just as the sun came peaking up over the plains one morning, I rousted carloads of kids to go with me to help Omdahl and his team do a four-city campaign blitz, going door-to-door and getting the word out about how great our guy was and what a dirty, rotten scoundrel our opponent was. I don't even remember the Republican's name. But it didn't matter. He was a Republican.

While I was in college at the University of North Dakota, I was president of the North Dakota Young Democrats as well as student body president. I campaigned for any and all Democrats that needed help. My favorite was George McGovern's presidential campaign. After all, we were fighting against the mother of all political mischief—Richard Milhaus Nixon. We may have lost, but we went down swinging.

In 1982 I ran for the North Dakota legislature against a college administrator. I thought I might one day run for governor. But I lost. In retrospect, it was a good thing. It suddenly dawned on me that my head was stuffed with theory, ideology, slogans, and an ego the size of Mount Rushmore. I needed some real world experience. I needed to figure out what I really believed and why. I needed to make some money for my new bride and family. So even though I'd studied journalism and political science in college, I accepted a job in Minneapolis in May of 1984—as a stockbroker for Paine Webber.

Stockbroker?! I know. It seems odd. A virtual Farmers Union communist from Main Street becoming a shill for the powerbrokers on Wall Street! Okay, I'll admit it wasn't exactly what my parents expected me to do. It wasn't what I expected to do. But, hey, it was a job. And it turned out to be fun. And I turned out to be good at it. And I was doing good things for others. I was helping people save and invest for the future, for their retirement. I was helping families turn a little into a lot. How bad is that?

In 1989, I was hired by a company in Connecticut, American Skandia, a mere two-year-old American division of a global financial services company based in Sweden and founded back in the nineteenth century. I became the twenty-fourth employee and the national sales manager at the corporate headquarters in Shelton, Connecticut. When I began, we had no wholesalers, no assets under management, and no sales whatsoever. So I hired people and got them selling financial products. Within two months, we'd passed our first million dollars in sales. By year's end, sales hit $6 million. By 1999 sales hit $10.1 billion. Today, we have more than $30 billion in client assets under management and more than 1,300 employees.

American Skandia's enormous growth and success over the past decade has tracked directly with the huge surge in interest in retirement planning and stock market investments by Baby Boomers recognizing how close they're getting to age sixty-five. As a Boomer at forty myself, I know full well where my nearly eighty million fellow Boomers are heading. I know why they're anxious about the Social Security system, why they're growing confident in the wealth-creating track record of the U.S. financial system, and why they're increasingly open to new ways to make the two systems work hand in hand. I know because I'm listening to the marketplace, as too many leaders in my party are not.

Fortunately, there are some exceptions, some leaders amidst the lost, who are laboring intensively to help my Democratic Party— the "party of the people"—find its voice once again on such a critical issue as Social Security.

One such hero is a man by the name of Sam Beard. Beard, a lifelong Democrat, became a believer in the power of personal retirement accounts in the early 1990s, after more than three decades in the field of urban economic development. In the 1960s Beard served as an advisor to then-New York Senator Robert Kennedy. He worked on the 1965 economic renewal program for Bedford-Stuyvesant, one of America's worst slums, located in Brooklyn, New York. After Kennedy was brutally and tragically cut down by an assassin's bullet, Beard founded the National Development Council, a national nonprofit organization created to help develop other local, inner-city economies. In this capacity, Beard would go on to serve as an urban economic development advisor to four U.S. presidents, Republicans and Democrats alike: Richard Nixon, Gerald Ford, Jimmy Carter, and Ronald Reagan. He helped raise more than $25 billion in private sector investments to help develop local, inner-city economies; arranged financing for more than 20,000 small businesses; helped create more than 500,000 private sector jobs, and helped more than 30,000 people learn the art of creating jobs, establishing credit, building relationships with local banks, and selecting and financing all kinds of business projects.

Along the way, Beard, who clearly knows how to help people in need, became convinced that economic development alone was not enough to raise people out of poverty. Something more was needed. Something that would help low-income people become financially independent. Something that would turn wages into wealth and workers into owners. But what? Around the time Bill Clinton was elected president in 1992, Beard began an intensive search for an answer to his dilemma, a search that would take him three full years. "I've gone all across the country and interviewed economists, Social Security and pension experts, historians, politicians, and political advisers," says Beard. "I've read hundreds of books and articles and turned the numbers upside down and inside out hoping to come up with an opening in the face of what seemed like an impenetrable wall. Piece by piece, a little at a time, the interviews, research, and calculations showed the way."

Beard started from FDR's original premise way back in 1935 that a worker's retirement security is a stool, resting on three legs. The first leg should be personal savings. The second leg should be a pension. The third and final leg should be a social safety net—Social Security—to keep retirees out of poverty. But Beard's research turned up some disturbing facts.

- Half of all Americans have $1,000 or less in personal savings.
- More than half of all Americans don't have their own pension plan (and many of those that do, have one that is grossly inadequate).
- Social Security is going broke—and the old ways of fixing it (raising taxes and cutting benefits) won't work.
- It takes money to make money—one-third of all income in America comes from capital, so those without any capital ownership are in danger of being left behind by those who do own capital and are, therefore, creating lasting, genuine wealth.

Now, Beard wondered, where could an American worker turn to find a big chunk of change with which to save and invest, create capital, create wealth, and thus augment his or her Social Security benefits? Where else, concluded Beard, but by being free to deposit a portion of his or her Social Security taxes into a personal retirement account and invest it in stocks, bonds, and mutual funds.

On August 14, 1995—the sixtieth anniversary of the Social Security system—the *Wall Street Journal* editorial page published an essay by Sam Beard. It was entitled "Minimum Wage Millionaires," and it represented the culmination of a three-year search—really, a three-decade-long search—for a way to help working families create wealth and financial independence. Beard wrote:

> Any American currently earning $10,000 a year pays $23.85 a week, or $1,240 a year, into Social Security. Imagine that, beginning at age 20, you invest that $23.85 a week at market rates. When you retire at age 65, you'll be a millionaire (before inflation). All that on minimum wage.... The plan keeps Social Security as a mandatory, redistributionist savings program but converts the program from the current pay-as-you-go system to a funded system, in which the individuals own retirement portfolios at Social Security and choose private investment managers. Individuals would be allowed to set aside portions of their Social Security payments, together with voluntary contributions, in their own personal accounts. They could use their accounts for retirement income and pass on the capital tax-free to their children...."

The essay was simple, powerful, and brilliant. It laid out the problem. It offered a positive, forward-looking solution. It even sketched out the transition to a new system of personal retirement accounts. What's more, it had been written by a life-long Democrat—a Bobby Kennedy advisor, of all people.

Beard went on to write a book and start a nonpartisan, national grassroots group called Economic Security 2000 to help spread the word about the power of personal retirement accounts to create wealth and retirement security for all workers. Along the way,

he recruited the help of Bob Kerrey, the senior Democratic senator from Nebraska, as an honorary co-chairman. Senator Kerrey
had delved deep into the impending collapse of Social Security as
co-chairman of the federal Entitlements Commission from 1994
through 1996 and, like Beard, had become increasingly convinced
that the old solutions wouldn't work—and that personal retirement accounts just might.

On April 15, 1997—tax day—Senator Kerrey published an
essay in the *Washington Post* entitled, "The Forgotten Tax." He
noted that while the federal income tax is certainly a real burden
on American workers and families, "the biggest tax burden is felt
not on this day but on every single day, when 12.4 percent of [a
worker's] wages are taken to provide retirement income for senior
citizens and operating revenue for the government." He called the
Social Security tax "super-regressive"—taxing everyone at the
bottom of the income scale and not taxing any income above
$65,400 (now the figure has climbed to over $72,000, but his
point remains valid).

What was Senator Kerrey's solution? "I have proposed a reform
under which families would invest two percentage points of what
they now pay into Social Security—2 percent of their income—in
Personal Investment Plans under their own control," Senator
Kerrey wrote. "These plans would provide a vehicle for building
retirement wealth....Moreover, some households not only lack a
stake in America's global success, but they are often the ones most
threatened by it. These are the families that see their wages stag-
nate and their jobs downsized while corporate profits—and the
wealth of those who own a stake—rise on each report of their
misery. Part of the solution is ensuring they have the skills to climb
the income ladder; another is ensuring laws are written so workers are treated fairly. The other part of the solution—just as vital—

is ensuring those workers own a stake in America's success."

Remarkably, Senator Kerrey—who, interestingly enough, as a presidential candidate in 1992 wasn't campaigning on proposals to create wealth but to create nationalized health care—became a leading advocate of Social Security Choice and personal retirement accounts. He wrote. He spoke. He debated. He worked the media. And he recruited yet another heavyweight, Daniel Patrick Moynihan, the senior senator from New York. Senator Moynihan has long been known as an Old Democrat, not a New Democrat, a man who vigorously opposed the 1996 welfare reform bill so popular with the rest of the country. So when Senator Moynihan began teaming up with Senator Kerrey—introducing legislation and talking publicly about a new approach to Social Security— heads began to turn. Mine certainly did.

The most amazing development to me came on May 30, 2000, when Senator Moynihan wrote an essay for the *New York Times* entitled "Building Wealth for Everyone," defending himself and Senator Kerrey against charges that they were trying to privatize Social Security. Amazing!

> Establishing personal savings accounts is described [by opponents, like Vice President Gore and the *New York Times*] as turning Social Security over to Wall Street. Dock workers would become day traders. A market downturn could wipe out benefits.
>
> The latter charge is obscene. The present progressive retirement benefit is fixed in our bill. There is no occasion to touch it. We add a savings plan modeled on the Thrift Savings Plan for federal employees, including senators. The government matches up to 5 percent of an employee's pay. The money is invested, at the employee's choice, in one of three plans, ranging from government bonds to a stock index fund. The employee can switch around from time to time. If there is an element of risk even in a forty-year stretch, at no time are basic Social Security benefits at risk. Those are fund-

ed and solid, just as they have been for sixty years.

The Thrift Savings Plan was essentially an adaptation of various retirement plans for federal workers, principally the 401(k), as it is known, which were passing the tax committees in the 1970s and 1980s. In the Senate, it emerged from the Government Affairs Committee. Al Gore, then a senator and a member of the committee, said on July 30, 1985, "An employee savings plan with government matching funds will give every worker the opportunity to supplement a defined and predictable pension amount." He praised a Congressional Research Service report, "Civil Service Retirement: Capital Accumulation Plans for Federal Employees."

A parallel arrangement under Social Security would, at a 7 percent non-inflation-adjusted rate of return, provide an average worker (making $30,000 a year), with $350,000 savings at the end of forty-five years. A measure of wealth.

In 1944, the British came up with the slogan of "cradle to grave" protection. We propose something beyond: an estate! For doormen, as well as those living in the duplexes above.

Clearly, the tide is beginning to turn within the ranks of the Democratic hierarchy. Visionaries such as Sam Beard, Sen. Bob Kerrey, and Sen. Daniel Patrick Moynihan understand the crisis Social Security faces, the burden it places on workers, and why personal retirement accounts—large or small—are such a powerful solution. It's not too late for the rest of my party to get on board. But let there be no doubt: If the Democratic Party—the "party of the people"—stands in the way of the financial security of some eighty million Baby Boomers and their children, it will be washed to sea like a castle made of sand. And it will deserve to be. Is this what FDR would have wanted? I sincerely doubt it.

Chapter Six

WORKERS OF THE WORLD, UNITE!

SO THERE YOU HAVE IT. We've looked at how you can retire as a millionaire—or close to it—without relying on Regis and why you should trust yourself, a professional financial advisor, and the pros on Wall Street rather than those in Washington to help you save and invest and retire with real financial security.

We've looked at the principles and key elements that any reform proposal worth its salt should encompass on the road to a new system of personal retirement accounts—namely, full protection of current and imminent retirees from any benefit cuts or tax increases and full freedom for younger workers to choose the plan that best meets their personal needs and financial goals.

We've looked at the eight reasons Social Security Choice is ultimately a more fair approach for working families as we enter the twenty-first century than the troubled system we have today.

We've also briefly examined the political lay of the land, how the GOP came to embrace personal retirement accounts, and why the Democratic Party—my party, the "party of the people"—

should embrace genuine Social Security Choice as the bold next step in preserving and perfecting FDR's cherished legacy.

Which brings me, finally, to my personal plea to the working families of this great country, the people who work hard and play by the rules, the people who make this country work by the sweat of their brow and the skill of their hands: It's your money, not Washington's—take control of it, don't let the politicians keep wasting and mismanaging it.

The issue isn't whether you work as a machinist in a factory or as an administrative assistant on the forty-first floor of a skyscraper. The issue isn't whether you're a teacher or a cop, a truck driver or a day care worker. The issue isn't whether you're a soccer mom or a Little League dad. Don't let the demagogues get you side-tracked.

The issue is whether you're a worker or an owner, a pawn or a player, a wage earner or a wealth-creator. The issue is whether the privileged few are going to be free to experience the miracle of the markets while you get left behind, or whether you, too, are going to be free to put a little of your own money—*your own money, for heaven's sake*—into an account that you own, that you manage, that you can watch grow, that you can pass on to your children and grandchildren, and that you can protect from the greedy hand of government. That's the issue.

This isn't about rich versus poor. The rich are already getting their fair share and then some. They'll be fine whether we reform Social Security or not. This is really about making sure working families don't get screwed by a sixty-five-year-old system riddled with financial mismanagement and structural flaws. This is really about making the necessary changes so that we can help the poor become middle class and the middle class become rich. This is really about helping you and your family fully participate in—and take advantage of—the greatest economic engine and bull market any country has ever created at any time in the history of mankind.

Look, you and I aren't a bunch of Robin Hoods. We're not communists or socialists. We're Americans. We're freedom fighters. We're rebels with a cause, and our cause is opportunity for all, responsibility from all. Our mission in life isn't to steal from the rich and give to the poor. Our mission in life, as a people, as a nation, is to make sure that all of us—young or old, black or white, Hispanic or Asian, Native American or any one of a gazillion other ethnicities and nationalities—are free to live our own lives, make our own choices, chart our own destinies, and pursue the opportunities that can lead us out of poverty and into prosperity. That's what America is all about. And that's what Social Security Choice is all about.

The interesting thing is that workers all over the world are beginning to realize that forking their money over to government isn't exactly a guarantee of true retirement security. They're beginning to realize that there really is a way to turn their wages into wealth. And they're beginning to insist upon the freedom to choose between a government promise and a personal retirement account they can own and manage themselves. It's time for us to do the same.

Take the workers of Chile, for example. In 1924 Chile became the first nation in the Western Hemisphere to adopt a government-run pension system. But after fifty-five years of government waste and mismanagement, the system began running out of money. So, on May 1, 1981, every worker in Chile was given the choice of either (1) remaining with the government-run pension system, with their benefits covered out of the government's general revenues or (2) putting a portion of their earnings in private pension accounts which were their own, beyond the reach of politicians.

The new system was the brainchild of a wonderfully innovative man by the name of Jose Piñera, then Chile's labor minister. "Why not the best system for everybody?" asked Piñera, who made regularly scheduled television appearances to explain the can't-lose proposal. He explained in simple, everyday terms—using props and familiar anecdotes and metaphors—that people would be permitted to invest in a range of safe, conservative, private investments such as mutual funds and bond funds that would provide a far better return on their money than the failing government-run system. He made a point of showing viewers a Social Security passbook—very much like a personal savings passbook—that would allow workers to see how much money was building up in their personal retirement account. And week after week, month after month, he stressed the fact that every worker would be free to choose—no one would be forced into a system with which he or she wasn't comfortable. Piñera's proposal proved to be a huge hit. Once Chilean workers had the freedom to choose, 94 percent of them opted to put their money in their own retirement accounts.

Piñera, now president of the International Center for Pension Reform, reported: "After fifteen years of operation, the results speak for themselves. Pensions in the new private system already are 50 to 100 percent higher—depending on whether they are old age, disability, or survivor pensions—than they were in the pay-as-you-go system. The resources administered by the private pension funds amount to $30 billion, in a country of only fourteen million people and a gross domestic product of only $70 billion." This boost in savings has, in turn, fueled phenomenal economic growth, benefiting everyone. In fact, notes Piñera, "The average worker has earned 12 percent annually after inflation," far above the pathetically poor 1 percent to 2 percent annual rate of return American workers earn through the current Social Security system. In the process, Piñera notes, the new system of Social Security Choice has helped every worker gain his or her own stake in the economic growth and well–being of the country.

Success breeds success. Chile's neighbors were the first to notice that something good was happening. Thus, in 1993 Peru began to give its workers more freedom and control over their retirement planning and savings, and Argentina followed suit the next year. American Nobel prize-winning economist Gary S. Becker has observed that "Argentina's experience demonstrates that, even under very difficult circumstances, a nation can successfully convert from a pay-as-you-go social security system to a competitive private pension plan with individual retirement accounts....The [new] program gives workers the option of either remaining in the old system or placing their old-age contributions into one of many private pension companies."

Other Latin American countries have also moved toward new systems of Social Security Choice, including Colombia, Bolivia, Mexico, and El Salvador. Each of these reforms has proved unbelievably popular. Carlos Bolona, the finance minister who implemented a privately run pension system in Peru, reported, "What the workers of Peru found compelling was the following message: 'We want to return your savings to you. The savings are yours, and the government has taken them from you and misused them for too long.'" Two years after Mexico gave people freedom of choice in 1997, for instance, 14.5 million Mexican workers took advantage of it. They deposited $15 billion with private pension managers, and this is expected to grow to over $130 billion by 2015.

In Europe, workers in Great Britain are benefiting from a system of Social Security Choice developed in 1986 by then Prime Minister Margaret Thatcher. "We have persuaded the bulk of the people to build up pension funds for retirement," wrote Peter Lilley, a British member of Parliament, in a 1999 study for the Washington, D.C.–based Heritage Foundation. "We allow and encourage them to opt out of the central government's State Earnings Related Pension Scheme (SERPS) into company or personal funds (like American Individual Retirement Accounts). Around 60 percent of those eligible do opt out.... Significantly, the total value of British-owned pension funds is now some $1.3 trillion. That is not just more than any other country in Europe. It is more than all the other countries in Europe put together have saved and invested for their own pension needs."

Now workers in Poland, too, are embracing Social Security Choice. Workers contribute 9 percent of their pay into retirement accounts and choose among investment managers. Some have been set up by the Catholic Church, some by Polish/Western joint ventures, and some by Solidarity and other trade unions. The Cato Institute's Andrew Biggs reports, "Polish workers can now tie their retirement savings to the higher rates of return obtainable in the market... if Polish workers receive average rates of return they could well end up with larger retirement incomes than many American workers will receive from a foundering Social Security system. And unlike the old Polish program—and Social Security— the new system affords each worker a property right in her pension. No one can take it away from her."

Indeed, Biggs adds, "It is a rich irony that a former member of the Warsaw Pact and one-time adversary of the West trusts its citizens to invest their retirement savings with financial giants such as Citibank, Aetna, Credit Lyonnais, and Allianz, while the U.S. government traps workers in a system promising only higher taxes and lower benefits. Poles may once have been the object of jokes, but when it comes to retirement security, it is they who may end up with the last laugh."

If everything goes well in Poland, it will set an influential example in Eastern Europe. The idea of a private pension system is being debated in Russia, and interest is growing in Hungary and Romania. Indeed, now even the government of China is beginning to look at a variation of personal retirement accounts to solve its massive and mounting retirement pension problems in a land of well over one billion people.

My point is that the global revolution for Social Security Choice has begun, and now it's our turn. Why should American workers be left behind when the workers of Great Britain and Chile have real choices and are creating real wealth?

Yes, many Democrat leaders and union leaders and other special interest group leaders may bitterly oppose Social Security Choice. But one by one, American workers and their families are coming to embrace such "bold, persistent experimentation."

A March 1999 survey by respected pollster John Zogby showed that 69 percent of Americans would be likely to support a new Social Security system if it allowed them to take their Social Security taxes and invest them in a retirement account of their own choosing. Only 30 percent of Americans were opposed. But even more interesting was this number: 66 percent of union members surveyed said they supported Social Security reform that let them use personal retirement accounts, while only 34 percent opposed such a reform. Imagine that: two out of three union members want more freedom and control, regardless of what the powers-that-be say. That says to me that the revolution isn't just global; it's local—and it's about to sweep change in and status quo thinking out.

Now it's up to you and me. Will we be silent, or will we insist on more control over our own money? Will we daydream about winning a million dollars on national TV with Regis Philbin, or will we begin to turn our own wages into real wealth? Will we entrust our future to next weekend's Powerball numbers, or will we demonstrate the vast political power of our vast and growing numbers? Will we let the demagogues rule the night, or will we seize the day? This is our moment. It's time to stand up, speak out, and vote our moral, financial, and generational interests, regardless of the political party to which perhaps we've always belonged. As a Baby Boomer, a lifelong Democrat, and someone who's invested his entire professional life to helping people turn a little into a lot, I say, "Workers of the world, unite! It's time to make Social Security Choice a glittering reality for every worker and every family!"

And that, Regis, is my final answer.

Resources

_____

DON'T SIMPLY TAKE MY WORD FOR IT. As the debate over Social Security Choice heats up, it will be essential for you to have access to the best research and analysis from both sides of the debate, those in favor *and* those opposed to personal retirement accounts.

Claims and counter-claims, accusations and counter-accusations—and a gazillion budget and economic numbers supporting both sides—will be flying about. Who will you believe?

Worse, the media will tend to underreport (and sometimes misrepresent) the facts. Reporters prefer hot, emotional clashes of personalities to cool, considered clashes of ideas. They prefer political junk food to policy health food, and this will make your job as a consumer of news and a participant in this historic debate all the more difficult.

That's why I've included this appendix, so you can quickly and easily find what the real experts are saying, draw your own conclusions, and make your own choice.

It is important to say here that I don't necessarily agree with all the views expressed by the proponents of Social Security Choice.

Nor do I necessarily agree with all the other views they express on other issues. At the same time, I should note that some of the opponents of Social Security Choice are friends of mine, and while I may disagree with them on this issue, I agree with them on others. The important thing is that both sides should be heard, whether you and I agree with them or not.

Note: This is a sampling of useful web sites. It is by no means complete.

ONE STOP SHOPPING

WWW.NEWCENTURYNEWDEAL.COM—As the Social Security Choice debate unfolds, I've created a web site to connect you with the latest research and analysis. All the links you see below are available here.

SUPPORTERS OF SOCIAL SECURITY CHOICE

WWW.ECONOMICSECURITY2000.ORG—This is the site run by Economic Security 2000, a group made up largely of Democrats like Sam Beard, Sen. Bob Kerrey and the like who advocate Social Security Choice and personal retirement accounts.

WWW.SOCIALSECURITY.ORG—This site is run by the Cato Institute, a public policy research organization in Washington, DC, and one of the leading proponents of personal retirement accounts. The group's main web site can be found at www.cato.org.

WWW.SOCIALSECURITY.ORG/CALC/CALCULATOR.HTML—Want to find out how much money you could retire with if you had a personal retirement account versus how much Social Security may pay you (if it doesn't go broke first)? This is the site. Here you can find a Social Security benefits calculator developed by the policy experts at Cato and the accounting experts at the respected firm of KPMG Peat Marwick.

WWW.SOCIALSECURITYREFORM.ORG—This site is run by the Heritage Foundation, a public policy research organization in Washington, DC, another leading proponent of personal retirement accounts. Among other features, it has a Social Security calculator. More detailed Social Security policy analysis can be found at www.heritage.org/library/socialsecurity.html. Their main web site can be found at www.heritage.org.

WWW.DLC.ORG—This site is run by the Democratic Leadership Council, a group of middle-of-the-road Democrats who support personal retirement accounts, among other pro-growth policies.

WWW.PENSIONREFORM.ORG—This is the web site run by the International Center for Pension Reform, led by Jose Piñera of Chile.

WWW.RETIRESECURE.ORG—This site is run by the Alliance for Worker Retirement Security, a group of citizen and business groups advocating Social Security Choice.

WWW.UNITEDSENIORS.ORG—This site is run by the United Seniors Association, a huge grassroots group of senior citizens committed to Social Security Choice.

WWW.60PLUS.ORG—This site is run by 60 Plus, another grassroots seniors group advocating Social Security Choice.

WWW.THIRDMIL.ORG—This site is run by Third Millennium, a group of Gen Xers committed to Social Security Choice.

WWW.NCPA.ORG—This site is run by the National Center for Policy Analysis, a public policy research center in Dallas, TX, that supports Social Security Choice.

WWW.CSE.ORG—This site is run by Citizens for a Sound Economy, a grassroots organization with chapters all over the country committed to Social Security Choice.

OPPONENTS OF SOCIAL SECURITY CHOICE

I believe so strongly that Social Security Choice is the way to go that I am not afraid of the challenges made by its opponents. In fact, I encourage you to do some "opposition research." I am confident that after considering the arguments against Social Security Choice, you will find them less persuasive than the arguments supporting it.

WWW.AFLCIO.ORG/SOCIALSECURITY/INDEX.HTM—This web site opposing Social Security Choice is part of a broader web site run by the country's largest labor unions, the AFL-CIO (www.aflcio.org). If you go specifically to www.aflcio.org/socialsecurity/links.htm—you'll see a long list of links to the web sites of various groups around the country, most of whom passionately oppose Social Security Choice.

WWW.SOCSEC.ORG—This site is run by the Social Security Network, a project of the Century Foundation. It contains a study, widely publicized by the Gore2000 campaign, critical of Social Security Choice.

WWW.CBPP.ORG—This site is run by the Center on Budget and Policy Priorities, a public policy group based in Washington, DC, one of the leaders in the fight against Social Security Choice.

WWW.OURFUTURE.ORG—This site is run by The Campaign for America's Future, and contains a section called the "Social Security Superpage."

HTTP://THENATION.COM/ISSUE/990208/0208DREYFUSS.SHTML —This link will take you directly to *The Nation* magazine's cover story opposing Social Security Choice which I refer to in chapter five.

WWW.NCSCINC.ORG/ISSUES/SS.HTM—This site is run by the National Council of Senior Citizens, a group that strongly opposes Social Security Choice.

WWW.NCPSSM.ORG—This site is run by the National Council

for the Preservation of Social Security and Medicare, a group that strongly opposes Social Security Choice.

WWW.PROSPECT.ORG—This site is run by *Prospect* magazine, a journal that has run articles strongly opposed to Social Security Choice.

WWW.PERSEUSBOOKSGROUP.COM/FEATURES/SKIDMORE1.HTML —Here you can buy a book entitled, *Social Security and Its Enemies* by Max J. Skidmore of the University of Missouri.

OFFICIAL GOVERNMENT WEB SITES

WWW.SSA.GOV—This is the U.S. federal government's official web page for the Social Security Administration. One particularly interesting section is a series of pages on the history of Social Security, www.ssa.gov/history/history.html.

WWW.CBO.GOV—This is the Congressional Budget Office's official web site. Here you'll find all kinds of useful economic and budget analyses, including the latest Social Security budget surplus projections.

Acknowledgments

THERE ARE MANY DAUNTING CHALLENGES IN LIFE. Only the most arrogant of people believe they can navigate without the guidance and assistance of friends, family and supporters. Blessedly, I am not one of them, though I struggle every day simultaneously not to fail as a friend, a husband, a father, an employee, or as a boss. On most days, I feel the verdict is mixed.

From the day the Cato Institute and my friend Steve Moore first brought me into the debate over Social Security Choice over four years ago, I slowly came to realize the full gravity of the issue at hand. The financial significance of the impending shortfall alone would make this the defining public policy issue of our time. We will be remembered, and our society will be profoundly shaped, by the policies we enact and the timeliness with which we enact them. The clock is ticking and society's judgement awaits.

I would also like to acknowledge the excellent writing of William Shipman and Pete Peterson. Both men have authored exceptional books on the subject of the public policy challenges to America posed by the maturing baby boomers, in particular the threat to Social Security. Along with Michael Tanner and Peter Ferrara, they are the men who have written most recently and most compellingly of the grave consequences our nation faces if it does not adequately address this problem.

My idea to draft an accessible set of ideas around Social Security reform first took hold over three years ago. However, the demands of my job and my young family delayed the project's start and would have prevented any progress whatsoever were it not for the untiring help of so many committed friends and associates.

The complex process of shepherding me through the research, the publishing, the editing, and all the other things relevant to the successful completion of a book has been carried on the shoulders of a brilliant young man. Without Jeremy Hildreth, there would not be a book. I cannot thank him enough for helping see this project to completion. My dream would be just that without his vision and his energy.

My emphatic intention for this book was to create a voice that would resonate with simplicity and informality. Social Security is a program for the entire American electorate, so a book positioned as a public policy "white paper" would fail to reach out to the American audience I seek. Joel Rosenberg, through his passion for this cause, and his ear for the language of today's culture, has helped me beyond any of my expectations to shape this voice. His knowledge of both the existing Social Security program and his years of passionate campaigning for a new one shine through on every page.

Much of the historical research on Social Security and the shaping of my initial arguments were accomplished with the gifted assistance of a true friend of liberty and freedom, Jim Powell. His work was immeasurable and his intellectual focus unwavering.

Jim is a gifted author and an extraordinary man. His patience, determination, and conviction served as the bedrock of the earliest work on the book.

Books need publishers, and books on Social Security need publishers more than most. The courage of Al Regnery to support books with a limited audience and books that tackle the most important issues of our body politic, however controversial, is highly laudable. I have the deepest gratitude for the risk he has assumed in publishing this book.

Then there is of course my friend and former associate Lawrence Kudlow. Intelligent and ideological, passionate, and practical Larry cannot help but to deeply influence those who's lives intersect with his. And while my politics and Larry's, in theory, should never cross, in reality they often do. I feel comfortable that in this book I have moved far closer to his sacred beliefs. It is for the long talks we've had and our longstanding relationship that I give him thanks.

Many have freely given their time and energy to assist the development of this book, to dig up research, and to help polish the many rough edges of the maturing document. To each I am deeply grateful. Carrie Lips, formerly with Cato and now at Harvard, laid the cornerstone of the underlying research product. Bill Beach and Gareth Davis of the Heritage Foundation shared their ideas, research insight, and data. Christine Hall in Congressman Mark Sanford's office obtained some obscure historical perspectives. Lianchau Han from Senator Rod Grams' office also aided in providing the historical context for Social Security.

The manuscript benefited from the critical assessment of early drafts by several well-respected experts and scholars: Mike Tanner of the Cato Institute and Peter Ferrara of Americans for Tax

Reform, authors of *A New Deal for Social Security*, a comprehensive look the Social Security challenge; Andrew Biggs, also at Cato, read drafts and a contributed research; Richard Thau of Third Millennium dedicated his personal time to that which he dedicates his professional time—the communication of this national threat; important to me in so many ways, as a valued critic, a dear friend of twenty years, a former employer, a grandfather to my children, the father of my wife, and a contributor to this book, Dr. Kent Alm.

So many others have supported my work or supported others who were part of this process. My humble thanks is extended to Bob Whitcher for his guidance, counsel, and insight. Diana Supersano for her tireless energy, unwavering support, and random acts of kindness. Kim Sembiante and Mary Gloersen each keep me pointing in the right direction and on the correct mission. Without these people I would be both lost and a lesser person.

This book and my professional life constantly call for amassing data and formulating it into a cogent message. The craft of understanding these challenges and the intellectual gifts necessary to assess the subject and the audience fall on the shoulders of Erik Gronvold. Without him, my ideas would be a jumble of words and white screens, begging for color and shape.

Several other close friends and associates have helped assess the work in progress. I thank each individually and commit that I will do the same when their own books are ready hit the shelves. Michael Murray who has so little time, gave generously to help shape the tone and direction. Marianne Stochmal also committed herself to ferreting out the weak elements. Jeffrey Jennes attacked the drafts from the important consideration of the potential investor perspective. Lastly, thanks to Lee Faragosa for her help with graphics and design.

There are two beautiful people still living upon the land my great grandmother from Norway homesteaded in Towner, North Dakota. They are tougher than I, having enjoyed some 140-odd Dakota winters between the two of them. June and Adrian Dokken raised me on local district political meetings, strong beliefs about the obligation of social and political participation, and the conviction that every vote matters. I still believe public service is a noble calling and I am grateful to all who give of themselves in dedicated service to our country.

And as I sit writing this final element of the book, I am drawn to give thanks to the woman who has given of herself in all that I could ask, more than I could dream, and always exceeding that which I deserve. A life is not a life unless it is shared by someone you love so deeply you cannot imagine life in any other way. The bounty with which God has graced my life up to this point all revolves around my love of twenty years, Susi Ann, and the three sons, Andrew, Chad, and Blake, that we share together.

Index

Gore, Tipper, 104
Gospel According to Regis, 20, 22, 94
government: central, 67; minimum benefit guarantee by, 40; personal retirement accounts and, 44; promises made by, 33, 60–63; socialist, 67; Social Security and, 11; society and, 16; spending by, 74–75
Government Affairs Committee, 118
Great Britain. *See* England
Great Depression, 13, 29, 54, 73
Greenspan, Alan, 42–43

Harlan, John, 63–64
Hart, Gary, 107
Harvard Business School, 28
Heritage Foundation, 87, 124, 129
Hispanic Americans, 87–88
Hispanic Business Roundtable, 87
Humphrey, Hubert, 110

income taxes, 34
Individual Retirement Accounts (IRAs), 13, 25, 124
individual stocks, 39
inflation, 56, 72
inheritance tax, 79
innovation, 71
International Center for Pension Reform, 122, 129
Internet, 39, 68, 108
investment: innovation and, 71; options for, 31, 39; personal retirement accounts and, 13, 36–37, 39; planning for, 26; of retirement money, 23, 56, 57–58; of Social Security, 42–43; in stock market, 21, 42, 100
IRAs (Individual Retirement Accounts), 13, 25, 124
Israel, 109

Janus Twenty Fund, 1
Johnson, Lyndon, 97
Jordan, Michael, 33
junk bonds, 39

Kaiser Family Foundation, 104, 105
Kennedy, John F., 78
Kennedy, Robert, 113
Kennedy School of Government, 104, 105
Kerrey, Bob, 59–60, 116, 118
Klein, Joe, 98
KPMG Peat Marwick, 128
Kudlow, Lawrence, 1, 135

Latin America, 67
Leach, Robin, 33
Leno, Jay, 108
Lieberman, Joe, 1
life insurance, 26, 40, 58
Lifestyles of the Rich and Famous, 33
Lilley, Peter, 124
Lynch, Peter, 25–26

Magellan Mutual Fund, 25–26
management: of finances, 26–27; of managers, 27–28; of personal retirement accounts, 26, 40
Marsico, Tom, 1
Marsico Capital Management, 1
Marx, Karl, 1
McCain, John, 101
McGovern, George, 111
McMahon, Ed, 64
Medicare, 74
men: lifespan of, 83; poverty among, 85
Mexico, 123
The Millionaire Mind, 20
The Millionaire Next Door, 20
minimum wage, 15
"Minimum Wage Millionaires" (Beard), 115